T0309316

# AMERICAN NATIONAL PARKS:
## CURRENT ISSUES AND DEVELOPMENTS

# AMERICAN NATIONAL PARKS:
## CURRENT ISSUES AND DEVELOPMENTS

### RONY MATEO
### EDITOR

**Novinka Books**
*New York*

**Senior Editors:** Susan Boriotti and Donna Dennis
**Coordinating Editor/Graphics:** Tatiana Shohov
**Office Manager:** Annette Hellinger
**Editorial Production:** Marius Andronie, Jonathan Boriotti, Robert Brower,
Maya Columbus, Matthew Kozlowski andLorna Loperfido
**Circulation:** Luis Aviles, Raymond Davis, Magdalena Nuñez, Marlene Nuñez,
Melissa Diaz, Jeannie Pappas, Vera Popovic and Frankie Punger
**Communications and Acquisitions:** Serge P. Shohov

*Library of Congress Cataloging-in-Publication Data*


ISBN: 1-59454-084-5.



Copyright © 2004 by Novinka Books
        Nova Science Publishers, Inc.
        400 Oser Ave, Suite 1600
        Hauppauge, New York 11788-3619
        Tele. 631-231-7269     Fax 631-231-8175
        e-mail: Novascience@earthlink.net
        Web Site: http://www.novapublishers.com

*Printed in the United States of America*

# CONTENTS

# PREFACE

The 108th Congress is considering legislation and oversight on many National Park Service related issues. The Administration also continues to address park and recreation issues through budgetary, regulatory, and other actions. Several key issues are covered in chapter one.

The National Park System includes 388 diverse units administered by the National Park Service (NPS) of the Department of the Interior (DOI). The resources of those units are to be preserved unimpaired for future generations. Units generally are added to the National Park System by act of Congress, although the President may proclaim national monuments on federal land for inclusion in the system. Before enacting a law to add a unit Congress might first enact a law requiring the NPS to study a prospective area, typically to assess its national significance and other factors. The Secretary of the Interior is required to prepare annually for Congress a list of areas recommended for study, as certain lists of areas previously studied. Significant areas also can be preserved outside the National Park System through programs managed or supported by NPS. Chapter two discusses these issues.

On July 31, 1997, the Environmental Protection Agency proposed a new regulatory program to reduce "regional haze." The proposed program would require the states to develop and implement long-term strategies to attain a congressionally mandated goal of remedying the impairment of visibility in national parks and wilderness areas resulting from man-made air pollution. Chapter three examines this program.

In chapter four the National Park System-wide closures are discussed. They result from recent government budgetary shutdowns and provoked intense complaints, from would-be visitors, and, particularly from financially affected local businesses that lost significant holiday-season business. Legislation to allow state employees to temporarily operate units of the national parks during periods of government budgetary shutdown is being considered by Congress.

On August 12, 1996, nearly six years after Crown Butte Resources, Ltd., submitted its operating plan for the proposed New World gold mine, its owners suspended permitting activities for the project. A "property exchange" agreement between Crown Butte and the U.S. government was reached under which the U.S. government would trade other federal lands, valued at $65 million, for Crown Butte's New World property interest. Chapters five and six examine the project.

Mineral development is often incompatible with other activities in National Park Service (NPS) units. Chapter seven illustrates how these conflicting land uses evolved, explains how landmark national park and wilderness legislation has impacted the issue, and provides a compendium of rules and regulations applied to mining in NPS units.

There are currently 690 natural and cultural sites from around the world on the World Heritage List, including twenty U.S. sites. The World Heritage in Danger List currently has 30 sites worldwide, including Yellowstone National Park and Everglades National Park. Chapter eight discusses the World Heritage List and recent issues of concern.

The Park Service reported that it incurred from $39 million to $50 million, in inflation-adjusted dollars annually, on travel costs during the past 4 fiscal years, but it does not know its actual costs for foreign travel or the travel costs related to attending conferences because its does not routinely record this required information. The Federal Travel Regulation requires that agency travel accounting systems capture certain data, including travel type, such as foreign or domestic travel, and purpose, such as training or conference attendance. In addition, the Park Service requires that all vouchers for foreign travel be processed at its Accounting Operations Center, but this policy is not consistently followed. The current procedures for processing travel vouchers and recording travel costs make it difficult for the Park Service to report reliable travel data that are consistent with the Federal Travel Regulation. Officials at the Park Service told us that they are implementing a new travel management system that will track travel type and purpose. The system is expected to be operating throughout the agency by approximately September 2003. Reliable, detailed travel information that is consistent with the Federal Travel Regulation is critical so that the Park Service and the Congress can perform their respective roles and responsibilities with regard to efficient travel cost management.

In chapter nine the GAO assesses the availability of travel cost information and provide certain travel cost information, such as the cost of foreign travel and for attending conferences, for the Park Service for each of the past 4 fiscal years.

In 2002, GAO reported that the design of the National Park Service's new asset management process was complete but implementation was just beginning. The new process will address deferred maintenance, commonly referred to as the maintenance backlog, as part of a much broader approach to its asset management. When fully developed and implemented, the new process will, for the first time, enable the agency to have a (1) reliable inventory of its assets; (2) process for reporting on the condition of the assets in its inventory; and (3) consistent, systemwide methodology for estimating the deferred maintenance costs for its assets. As a result, agency managers and the Congress should receive much more accurate and reliable information on the amount of deferred maintenance needs throughout the national park system. Nonetheless, while the Park Service's current efforts are promising, GAO reported on a few areas that the agency needed to address to improve the performance of the process. These included the need to (1) develop costs and schedules for completing the implementation of the process, (2) better coordinate the tracking of the process among Park Service headquarters units to avoid duplication of effort within the agency; and, (3) better define its approach to determine the condition of its assets, and how much the assessments will cost. Since that report, the agency appears to have made progress. While the complete implementation of the process will not occur until fiscal year 2006, the agency has completed, or is nearing completion of, a number of substantial and important steps. According to the Park Service, the agency has completed its asset inventory and trained staff on the use of the required computer software. In addition, the Park Service provided information indicating that it was addressing each of the concerns identified in GAO's 2002 report. Specifically, the Park Service (1) developed cost and schedule estimates for the complete implementation of the process, (2) developed a plan with an implementation schedule to eliminate any duplication or inconsistencies between organizational components, and (3) completed annual condition assessments--visual inspections--on all but nine of the larger parks in the system for which it only plans to perform a more comprehensive condition assessment. According to the Park Service, the work done so far are necessary steps and reflect some of the best practices of the private sector in developing and implementing an effective facility management process.

GAO, the Department of the Interior, and others have reported on the National Park Service's efforts to develop an effective maintenance management process that would, among other things, enable the agency to accurately and reliably estimate the amount of deferred maintenance on its assets. Over the years, the agency's estimates of the cost of its deferred maintenance have varied widely--sometimes by billions of dollars. Currently, the agency estimates that its deferred maintenance backlog will cost over $5 billion. In April 2002, GAO reported on the status of efforts to develop better deferred maintenance data. Chapter ten presents the results of GAO's April report and updates the progress the Park Service is making in implementing its new asset management process.

The Everglades, a unique network of subtropical wetlands, is now half its original size. Many factors have contributed to its decline, including flood control projects and agricultural and urban development. As part of a larger restoration program for South Florida, the U.S. Army Corps of Engineers (Corps) and other federal, state, tribal, and local agencies collaborated to develop a Comprehensive Everglades Restoration Plan (CERP or the plan). CERP focuses on increasing storage of wet season waters to provide more water during the dry season for both the natural system and urban and agricultural users. The plan consists of 68 projects estimated to take more than 30 years and $7.8 billion to complete. The Water Resources Development Act of 2000 (P.L.106-541) authorizes appropriations for initial construction projects and their operation and maintenance. The federal government will pay half the plan's costs and an array of state, tribal, and local agencies the other half. Major issues associated with the plan include timely completion of restoration, phosphorous mitigation implementation of programmatic regulations, effectiveness of restoration efforts, coordination of efforts, uncertainties in technologies and costs, and effect on the Corps budget. Chapter eleven outlines the history and current conditions of the Everglades, CERP legislation and funding, and associated issues.

*Chapter 1*

# NATIONAL PARK
# MANAGEMENT AND RECREATION*

## *Carol Hardy Vincent*

### ABSTRACT

The 108th Congress is considering legislation and conducting oversight on many National Park Service (NPS) related issues. The Administration also continues to address park and recreation issues through budgetary, regulatory, and other actions. Several key issues are covered in this chapter.

## Maintenance Backlog

There is debate over the funding level to meet the physical maintenance obligations of the land management agencies and whether to provide new funds or use funds from existing programs for them. Attention has focused on the NPS's multi-billion dollar maintenance backlog. President Bush set out to eliminate that backlog by FY2006. Congress included money for some maintenance backlog needs in the FY2003 Interior appropriations law and FY2004 appropriations bills.

---

* Excerpted from CRS Report IB10093. Updated September 5, 2003.

## Personal Watercraft and Snowmobiles

Motorized recreation, notably the use of personal watercraft (PWC) and snowmobiles in NPS units, has fueled debate over the balance between recreation on, and protection of, park lands. Regulatory actions that restrict use of these vehicles are particularly controversial. The NPS currently is evaluating PWC use in some areas. A February 2003 NPS plan allows snowmobile recreation to continue in Yellowstone and Grand Teton National Parks and the John D. Rockefeller, Jr., Memorial Parkway.

## Aircraft Overflights

Grand Canyon National Park is at the center of a conflict over whether to limit air tours over national parks to reduce noise. The NPS and the Federal Aviation Administration continue to work on implementing a 1987 law that sought to reduce noise at Grand Canyon as well as a 2000 law that regulates overflights at other park units. Recent regulations require air tour operators to seek authority to fly over park units, and the agencies then must develop Air Tour Management Plans at park units.

## Recreational Fee Demonstration Program

The "Fee Demo" Program was created to allow the NPS and other land management agencies to test the feasibility of supplemental self-financing through new fees. The Bush Administration supports making the program permanent, and Congress is considering related legislation as well as legislation to extend the program. P.L. 107-63 extended the program through FY2004 for fee collection and FY2007 for expenditures and gave agencies discretion to establish any number of fee projects, among other changes.

## The National Trails System

While designation of trails is often popular, issues remain regarding funding, expansion, and quality of trails. Congress is considering bills to amend the National Trails System Act to provide authority to acquire land from willing sellers for certain trails; to authorize studies of routes for possible additions to the System; and to add routes to the System.

## Heritage Areas

Congress has designated 23 National Heritage Areas whereby the NPS, through partnerships, supports state and local conservation of natural, scenic, historic, cultural, and recreational resources. The NPS provides technical and limited financial assistance to these areas, which remain in nonfederal ownership. A number of legislative initiatives are pending to study, designate, and fund heritage areas as well as to establish consistent criteria and a process for designating and managing these areas.

## MOST RECENT DEVELOPMENTS

On July 8, 2003, the National Parks Subcommittee of the Senate Committee on Energy and Natural Resources held a hearing to address the maintenance backlog of the National Park Service. The NPS has issued regulations to permit personal watercraft (PWC) use at Lake Mead National Recreation Area and Assateague Island National Seashore. Glen Canyon National Recreation Area released a record of decision on June 30, 2003, to allow PWC use at Lake Powell. An additional 13 areas remain closed to PWCs. All of them are pursuing a rulemaking process to eventually permit their use. Also, the NPS overturned a snowmobile ban in Yellowstone and Grand Teton National Parks and the John D. Rockefeller, Jr. Memorial Parkway; the March 2003 Record of Decision establishes daily snowmobile entry limits, requires trained guides, requires reservations for non-commercially guided groups, and implements best available technology standards for noise and emissions. Two lawsuits have been filed to overturn this decision and restore the phase-out. A conference report on H.R. 2115, filed July 25, 2003, directs the Secretary of Transportation to issue a final rule, no later than January 2005, establishing standards for quiet technology that are "reasonably achievable" at Grand Canyon National Park. H.R. 2691, as passed by the House, would extend the Recreational Fee Demonstration Program. On July 17, 2003, the Senate passed S. 651 to authorize land acquisition from willing sellers for specified trails. In addition, 32 bills are pending to study or designate new heritage areas, and another measure would establish a policy structure and consistent designation criteria.

# BACKGROUND AND ANALYSIS
## INTRODUCTION

The National Park System [http://www.nps.gov/legacy/] is perhaps the federal land category best known to the public. The National Park Service (NPS) in the Department of the Interior (DOI) manages 388 units, including 56 units formally entitled "national parks" and a host of other designations. The System has more than 84 million acres.[1] The NPS had an appropriation of approximately $2.25 billion in FY2003, employs about 21,000 permanent and seasonal employees, and uses an additional 90,000 volunteers. An estimated 276 million people visited park units in 2002. While high, this figure is a decline from the 1999 peak of about 287 million visitors. The decrease is attributed to a downturn in the economy as well as security concerns following the September 11, 2001 terrorist attacks on the United States. Security concerns led to a drop in international tourism and closure of NPS icons, such as the White House and the Statue of Liberty, which usually draw large numbers of visitors.

The NPS statutory mission is multi-faceted: to conserve, preserve, protect, and interpret the natural, cultural, and historic resources of the Nation for the public and to provide for their use and enjoyment by the public. The mission's dichotomy of use and preservation can sometimes be inherently contradictory. In general, activities which harvest or remove resources from units of the System are not allowed. The NPS also supports the preservation of natural and historic places and promotes outdoor recreation outside the System through grant and technical assistance programs. The emphasis is on cooperation and partnerships with state, municipal, and local governments as well as foundations, corporations, and other private parties to protect National Park System units and to advance NPS programs. Attention centers on how to balance the recreational use of parklands with the preservation of park resources, and on determining appropriate levels and sources of funding to maintain NPS facilities and to manage NPS programs.

---

[1] This figure includes an estimated 79 million acres of federal land, 1 million acres of other public land, and 4 million acres of private land. NPS policy is to acquire these non-federal "in-holdings" from willing sellers or to create special agreements to encourage land owners to sell.

# HISTORY

The establishment of several national parks preceded the 1916 creation of the National Park Service (NPS) as the park system management agency. Congress established the Nation's first national park — Yellowstone National Park — in 1872. The park was created in the then-territories of Montana and Wyoming "for the benefit and enjoyment of the people," and placed "under the exclusive control of the Secretary of the Interior" (16 U.S.C. §§21-22). In the 1890s and early 1900s, Congress created several other national parks mostly from western public domain lands, including Sequoia, Yosemite, Mount Rainier, Crater Lake, and Glacier. In addition to the desire to preserve nature, there was interest in promoting tourism. Western railroads, often recipients of vast public land grants, were advocates of many of the early parks and built grand hotels in them to support their business.

At the same time, there were efforts to protect the sites and structures of early Native American cultures along with other special sites. In 1906, Congress enacted the Antiquities Act to authorize the President to proclaim national monuments on federal lands that contain "historic landmarks, historic and prehistoric structures, and other objects of historic or scientific interest" (16 U.S.C. §431). Most national monuments are managed by the NPS.

There was no system of national parks and monuments until 1916, when President Wilson signed a law creating the NPS to manage and protect the national parks and many of the monuments then in existence and those yet to be established. That "Organic Act" provided that the NPS "shall promote and regulate the use of the Federal areas known as national parks, monuments, and reservations ... to conserve the scenery and the natural and historic objects and the wild life therein and to provide for the enjoyment of the same in such manner and by such means as will leave them unimpaired for the enjoyment of future generations" (16 U.S.C. §1). A major step in developing a national system of parks occurred in 1933, when President Franklin D. Roosevelt transferred 63 national monuments and historic military sites from the USDA Forest Service and the War Department to the NPS.

# OVERVIEW OF ISSUES

The 108th Congress is considering legislation or conducting oversight on many NPS-related issues. Several major issues are covered in this chapter: funding for the maintenance backlog of the NPS and other agencies, regulation of personal watercraft, use of snowmobiles, overflights of aircraft, extension of the Recreational Fee Demonstration Program, expansion of the National Trails System, and designation of heritage areas. While in some cases these issues are relevant to other federal lands and agencies, this chapter does not comprehensively cover issues primarily affecting other lands/agencies.

NPS-related issues not described in this brief include protection from outside threats, funding of the Land and Water Conservation Fund (LWCF), the creation of new park units, and funding for anti-terrorism activities. First, while parks historically were "buffered" from much human impact by their remote locations and adjoining wild lands, the situation has changed. How to protect park resources from outside threats such as detrimental land uses, growing populations, contaminated water, and tourist attractions, while at the same time recognizing the benefits of growth, development, and tourism to surrounding communities, presents difficult issues for Congress. Second, the LWCF is the principal federal source of money for the NPS (and other agencies) to acquire new recreation lands. Policy issues include the size of the fund, need for an annual appropriation, and the congressional role in choosing lands to acquire. Third, how national park units are created and what qualities make a potential area eligible to be an NPS unit are of continuing interest. Fourth, the NPS manages high profile natural and commemorative sites, including many of the monuments in Washington, DC, and is thus undertaking new security initiatives in response to the terrorist attacks of September 11, 2001. Congress determines the level of funding for anti-terrorist activities in appropriations laws.

# CURRENT ISSUES
# MAINTENANCE BACKLOG
# (BY CAROL HARDY VINCENT AND DAVID WHITEMAN)

## Background

The four federal land management agencies — the National Park Service, Bureau of Land Management (BLM), and Fish and Wildlife Service (FWS) in the Department of the Interior and the Forest Service (FS) in the Department of Agriculture — have extensive physical maintenance obligations involving buildings, roads, trails, recreation sites, and other infrastructure. There is debate over the levels of funds appropriate to maintain this infrastructure, whether to appropriate new funds or to use funds from existing programs, and the best balance between maintaining the existing infrastructure and acquiring new assets. The agencies, particularly the NPS and FS, assert considerable unmet maintenance needs, often called "deferred maintenance" or the "maintenance backlog" — essentially maintenance that could not be done when scheduled or planned. The estimate of deferred maintenance for the four agencies is $13.8 billion. The FS and the NPS together account for nearly 90% of the backlog, with the FS having the largest estimated share ($6.5 billion) and the NPS having the second largest ($5.4 billion). The FWS share is $1.5 billion, and the BLM backlog is the lowest ($0.4 billion). The backlogs have been attributed to decades of funding shortfalls. The agencies assert that deferred maintenance of facilities accelerates their rate of deterioration, increases their repair costs, and decreases their value.

Attention has centered on the NPS maintenance backlog. Concern about deteriorating NPS facilities led to increased overall NPS appropriations for each year from FY1996 to FY2002 and to new funding sources for the backlog. The Clinton Administration's FY2000 budget proposal first highlighted an Interior Department-wide campaign to identify priorities in maintenance needs over a 5-year period. For each year since, the NPS has submitted a Five Year Maintenance and Capital Improvement Plan identifying deferred maintenance projects by priority. An Interior Department Inspector General report (December 2001) recommended establishing a single maintenance budget funded through one appropriation for the entire department. In addition, many state park systems also have significant backlogs of maintenance and construction projects, and some states expect the problem to worsen due to cuts as a result of overall state budget shortfalls.

## Administrative Actions

The Bush Administration set out to eliminate the NPS backlog over 5 years. In FY2002, the President requested $4.9 billion over 5 years (FY2002 — FY2006) to eliminate that backlog through a combination of transportation fund money, appropriated funds, and revenues from recreation fees. For deferred maintenance the President requested $440 million yearly. Because the President's FY2004 budget combines funding for all NPS construction and regular and deferred maintenance ($706 million), it is unclear what amount is requested for deferred maintenance. The FY2004 combined request is a $58 million increase (9%) over FY2003 ($648 million) and a $24 million (3.5%) increase over FY2002 ($682 million). Neither the House-passed (H.R. 2691), nor Senate Appropriations Committee-reported (S. 1391), appropriations bill identifies the portion of funds for reducing backlogged maintenance.

On July 2, 2003, the National Park Service issued a report addressing the "significant progress" the Department has made in addressing the maintenance backlog of the National Park Service and other park issues [www.nps.gov/accompreport2003/]. The report states that the President "will fulfill his commitment to address the $4.9 billion maintenance backlog" of the National Park System and has spent $2.9 billion towards that goal. That figure includes money requested for FY2004. The National Parks Conservation Association, among others, disagrees that the Administration is on track to eliminate the backlog. The Association asserts that national parks "suffer from" an annual shortfall in operational funding of about 32%. It also asserts that the Administration has supported little new money to address park maintenance, and "has mostly manipulated existing accounts to support its claim to be on track to eliminate the backlog." (See: [www.npca.org/flash.html].)

The agencies are undertaking to define and quantify their maintenance needs. These efforts include improvement or development of computerized systems for tracking maintenance projects; prioritizing maintenance projects, with emphasis on critical health and safety and resource protection; and collecting comprehensive data on the condition of facilities, to more definitively identify maintenance needs. Without such data, the precise extent and nature of deferred maintenance might not be fully known, potentially hampering federal efforts to overcome the backlog.

## Legislative Activity

On July 8, 2003, the National Parks Subcommittee of the Senate Committee on Energy and Natural Resources held a hearing to address the maintenance backlog of the National Park Service. The hearing covered the Park Service's effort to assess the condition of all facilities, estimate costs of repairing facilities and total deferred maintenance, and determine maintenance priorities. The Park Service has acknowledged that until the effort is completed—by FY2006—it will not have the data to accurately estimate its maintenance backlog and assess the agency's success in eliminating it. Witnesses from the private sector testified that the backlog results from a lack of adequate funding for annual maintenance and that substantial additional funds are needed so that the backlog does not continue to grow. One witness asserted that there is also a large backlog in natural resource protection projects, such as elimination of invasive species.

On March 31, 2003, legislation was introduced to amend the Land and Water Conservation Fund to make the fund available to the Park Service and the other land management agencies for maintenance. The bill, H.R. 1517, requires that within 5 years these agencies reduce their backlogged maintenance by at least 20%. Additional reductions in backlogged maintenance are to be made during subsequent five year periods. The measure also requires the agencies to submit to Congress, every 5 years, reports on the progress made in reducing backlogged maintenance and on the priorities for construction and maintenance in order to reduce their backlogs.

## PERSONAL WATERCRAFT (BY KORI CALVERT)

## Background

PWCs are high-speed, very shallow draft, and highly maneuverable watercraft "operated by a person or persons sitting, standing, or kneeling on the vessel rather than within the confines of the hull" (36 CFR §1.4). Often used to perform stunt-like maneuvers, PWCs include watercraft known by their brand and generic names as jet ski, sea doo, surf jet, water sled, wavejammer, wetjet, waverunner, and wet bike. While PWCs represent a small segment of the recreational boat market, the number of PWC accidents has been an issue. Critics of motorized recreation cite environmental concerns, including noise, air, and water pollution; damage to land, plants, and wildlife; and public safety. Supporters of motorized access argue that technological advances will enable manufacturers to produce cleaner, more efficient machines, and point to the economic benefits to communities serving users. PWC users also assert that in park units that allow motorized boating generally, PWCs also should be allowed. Recent controversies have focused on regulatory actions that would restrict recreational use or "access" of these vehicles, often in specific park units.

## Administrative Actions

In an effort to manage PWC use, the NPS issued a rule (effective April 20, 2000) prohibiting PWC use from 66 of the 87 units where motorized boats were allowed (65 *Fed. Reg.* 15077). The rule allowed PWC use to continue until April 22, 2002, at the remaining 21 areas while the NPS evaluated whether to permanently authorize PWC use and develop special regulations. The rule recognized that PWC use might continue in certain National Recreation Areas (NRAs), such as Lake Mead and Glen Canyon, where the establishing legislation emphasized motorized water-based recreation as a primary purpose. The April, 2001 negotiated settlement of a lawsuit by Bluewater Network and Earth Island Institute over the PWC rule prohibited PWCs from the 21 areas unless the Park Service initiated park-specific rules and environmental analyses. PWCs could continue to operate during the rulemaking process, with a completion deadline of April 22, 2002, for 13 units and September 15, 2002, for 8 NRAs.

Of the 13 units with April 22, 2002 deadlines, the NPS prohibited PWC use in 5 units (effective April 22, 2002) that had completed an environmental review process and favored PWC bans: Cape Cod National Seashore, Delaware Water Gap NRA, Indiana Dunes National Lakeshore, Cumberland Island National Seashore, and Whiskeytown NRA. On April 19, 2002, a federal judge denied an injunction sought by PWC users and manufacturers to overturn these bans. The other 8 units closed to PWCs on April 22, 2002, and will remain closed until the environmental assessment and rulemaking process is completed. The 8 NRAs with the September 15, 2002 deadline were to close temporarily then if the public review process was not completed. However, on September 6, 2002, an agreement was filed in federal court that extended PWC use at these 8 NRAs through November 6,

2002, when the recreational boating season ended. The Lake Mead PWC ban subsequently was postponed until April 10, 2003. Final Lake Mead rules issued April 9, 2003 (68 *Fed. Reg.* 17292) authorize PWC use in 95% of the area's waters. Assateague National Seashore is reopening two small areas to PWC users (68 *Fed.Reg.* 3237ł), effective June 30, 2003. A May 2003 negotiated lawsuit settlement between NPS and a coalition of small business owners and recreational access groups lifted the PWC ban at Glen Canyon National Recreation Area's Lake Powell through September 30, 2003. NPS has completed the final environmental impact statement for that unit (68 *Fed.Reg.* 26645) and released a record of decision on June 30, 2003 [http://www.nps.gov/glca/plan.htm], [68 *Fed. Reg.* 43544]. The agency anticipates completing final rules this summer. PWCs continue to be banned in 13 other areas. All of these areas are working on environmental reviews and special regulations to allow PWC use. NPS does not expect the rulemaking process to be completed for most areas in time for the 2003 boating season.

## Legislative Activity

Legislation (H.R. 1831) to extend the grace period for PWC use in Glen Canyon National Recreation Area was introduced April 12, 2003. No action has been taken.

# SNOWMOBILES (BY KORI CALVERT)

## Background

On April 26, 2000, the NPS announced the strict enforcement of existing, long-standing regulations on snowmobile use which would have substantially reduced snowmobile use in those 42 national parks units that allowed recreational snowmobiling. Exceptions included Yellowstone and Grand Teton National Parks, park units in Alaska, Voyageurs National Park in Minnesota, and access to private land within or adjacent to a park. The snowmobile prohibition was both praised and reviled in the press and prompted several congressional hearings. By July 2000 the Interior Department had backed away from its strict enforcement stance — rather, there would be no snowmobile ban in park units pending formal rulemaking, which to date has not occurred for parks generally.

## Administrative Actions

Regulatory action to restrict or allow snowmobile use has centered on Yellowstone and Grand Teton National Parks and the John D. Rockefeller, Jr. Memorial Parkway. The Clinton Administration issued rules on snowmobile use in these areas (66 *Fed. Reg.* 7260, Jan. 22, 2001) that would phase out snowmobile use beginning with the start of the 2003/2004 winter season, with limited exceptions, and phase in a replacement of snowmobiles with multi-passenger "snow coaches." The Bush Administration announced in April 2001 that it would allow the rule to stand. The NPS delayed implementation until the end of the 2003-2004 winter use season (67 *Fed. Reg.* 69473, Nov. 18, 2002). Four environmental groups filed a lawsuit on December 3, 2002, to restore the snowmobile phase-out schedule under the Clinton rules.

Concurrently, the Administration continued to negotiate settlement of a lawsuit by the International Snowmobile Manufacturers Association and others to overturn the ban in these three areas and re-open the rulemaking process. The June 29, 2001 settlement agreement required NPS to prepare a supplemental environmental impact statement (66 *Fed. Reg.* 39197, July 27, 2001) on snowmobile use in these areas by early 2002, and to decide whether to keep or modify the ban by November 2002. The deadline for the record of decision was extended to March 15, 2003.

The NPS announced release of its final supplemental environmental impact statement on February 20, 2003 (*68 Fed. Reg.* 8616, Feb. 24, 2003). The NPS winter use plan outlined a controversial preferred alternative that allows continued snowmobile use within specific phased-in parameters. These include daily limits on snowmobile numbers; use of cleaner, 4-stroke engines; commercially-guided access for up to 80% of all snowmobiles; NPScertified guides and a reservation system for the remaining 20% non-commercial entries; development of snowcoach technology for winter transit; and monitoring of long- and shortterm effects of noise and pollution on park resources.

A Record of Decision (ROD) (see [http://www.nps.gov/grte/winteruse/winteruse.htm]) announced on March 25, 2003 finalized the snowmobile management plan with a few modifications, increasing daily entry limits to 1,140 from 1,100. Plan proponents characterize it as an attempt to achieve equilibrium between motorized and non-motorized recreational activities as it neither calls for a total snowmobile ban nor provides for unlimited numbers of snowmobilers. Opponents, however, note that the final winter use plan also identifies the alternative implementing the Clinton

Administration snowcoaches-only policy in the 2005-2006 winter season as the "environmentally preferred alternative." On August 27, 2003, NPS issued proposed regulations (68 *Fed. Reg.* 51526) to implement the ROD. Outlining an "adaptive management strategy," the rule allows park managers to take remedial action if park resource monitoring indicates unacceptable impacts from air and noise pollution. Actions could include adjustments to Best Available Technology requirements or daily entry limits, road closures, or timed entries.

Environmental groups filed 2 federal court challenges to the NPS final decision on March 25, 2003, seeking to overturn it and to halt winter road grooming until its impact on bison and other wildlife is determined. Yellowstone announced its 2003-2004 winter season snowmobile reservation system on July 10, 2003 [http://www.nps.gov/yell/press/0348.htm].

In related developments, on September 13, 2002, the U.S. Environmental Protection Agency (EPA) issued final regulations limiting air emissions from nonroad recreational vehicles (67 *Fed. Reg.* 68241). They require snowmobile manufacturers to reduce hydrocarbon and carbon monoxide emissions about 50% below current levels by 2012. Two environmental groups filed a lawsuit against EPA on January 7, 2003, claiming the standards do not meet Clean Air Act requirements.

## Legislative Activity

On a tie vote (210-210) on July 17, 2003, the House failed to approve an FY2004 Interior Appropriations amendment that essentially would have halted snowmobile use at Yellowstone and Grand Teton National Parks and John D. Rockefeller Memorial Parkway, as stipulated in the Clinton Administration rule. The Yellowstone Protection Act (H.R. 1130), introduced March 6, 2003, requires implementation of the Clinton Administration final rulemaking to phase out snowmobiles in Yellowstone and Grand Teton National Parks and John D. Rockefeller, Jr. Memorial Parkway. An identical bill (S. 965) was introduced May 1, 2003.

# AIRCRAFT OVERFLIGHTS (BY KORI CALVERT AND CAROL HARDY VINCENT)

## Background

Minimizing noise to protect the natural condition is an important element of the NPS mission to preserve natural resources and enhance visitor enjoyment. The Federal Aviation Administration (FAA) controls airspace and the aircraft overflights that may jeopardize a park unit's natural quiet, impair visitor enjoyment, and raise safety concerns. This creates a conflict between resource protection and aviation access authorities and their constituencies. ·

Grand Canyon National Park has been the focal point of the conflict between groups seeking to limit overflights and air tour operators whose economic stability, with ripple effects on local businesses, may depend on providing overflights. The National Parks Overflights Act of 1987 (P.L. 100-91) directed NPS to recommend a flight control plan for Grand Canyon that would provide a "substantial restoration of the natural quiet" and prohibited flights below the Canyon's rim. It also mandated an NPS study on the effects of all aircraft overflights, which was submitted to Congress in 1994. An October 3, 2002 Senate hearing explored why the Act has not been fully implemented.

The National Parks Air Tour Management Act of 2000 (Title VIII, P.L. 106-181) regulates commercial air tours at most other park units (exceptions include parks and tribal lands in Alaska). It requires the FAA and NPS to create management plans for air tours at individual park units and within a half mile of their boundaries. Each plan could prohibit or limit air tours, such as by route and altitude restrictions. The Act also requires the FAA to establish quiet aircraft technology standards for the Grand Canyon within one year and to designate Grand Canyon routes or corridors for aircraft and helicopters using quiet technology. Quiet aircraft would not be subject to existing caps on Canyon overflights.

## Administrative Actions

President Clinton directed the Secretary of Transportation to develop regulations to address the impacts of transportation, including overflights, on national parks (61 *Fed. Reg.* 18229, April 22, 1996). The President also set

2008 as the date to substantially restore natural quiet at Grand Canyon National Park. That mandate, and congressional directives, have segued into an ongoing and contentious rulemaking process. Controversial regulations include two FAA rules affecting Grand Canyon. The first one, a "limitations rule" that caps the annual number of commercial air tour overflights at Grand Canyon, took effect on May 4, 2000. An August, 2002 appeals court decision on the limitations rule directed the FAA to use NPS "natural quiet" standards and to consider commercial flight-generated noise impacts in developing air tour overflight regulations. This stricter standard is viewed as likely to lead to increased quiet at Grand Canyon. The Court simultaneously rejected a challenge by the air tour industry that the limitations rule is unlawful. The air tour industry seeks exemptions to air tour caps, as well as curfews and air route restrictions, if quiet aircraft technology is used.

The second rule, the "airspace rule," imposes increased flight-free zones and restrictive routing over the Canyon (65 *Fed. Reg.* 17736 and 17708, April 4, 2000). New routes and airspace restrictions for the Canyon's west end Special Flight Rules Area (SFRA) took effect April 19, 2001. To address air tour operators' safety concerns, east end SFRA airspace changes were delayed until February 20, 2003 (66 *Fed. Reg.* 63294). On February 27, 2003, the FAA issued a final rule (68 *Fed. Reg.* 9496) staying the east end changes until February 20, 2006, to resolve issues surrounding routes.

A third FAA action relates to Grand Canyon. On March 24, 2003, the FAA published a supplemental notice of proposed rulemaking (68 *Fed. Reg.* 14276) to establish a standard for quiet technology for certain aircraft in commercial air tour operations over Grand Canyon National Park. In defining quiet technology, the FAA proposes to use a noise efficiency approach, whereby larger aircraft with more seats for passengers are allowed to make proportionately more noise. Aircraft used for air tours would be categorized according to noise efficiency. The goal of the proposal is to help the NPS achieve its mandate (under P.L. 100-91) to provide for the substantial restoration of natural quiet at Grand Canyon, and to determine the role of quiet technology in that regard. Further, the proposal seeks to comply with an FAA mandate (under P.L. 106-181) to designate reasonably achievable requirements for aircraft to be considered as using quiet aircraft technology. The rule was open for public comment through June 23, 2003.

Other regulatory actions affect commercial air tours at park units generally. The FAA issued a National Parks Air Tour Management Act final rule (67 *Fed. Reg.* 65661, October 25, 2002,) to complete the definition of "commercial air tour operation." The rule requires air tour operators to apply for authority, by January 23, 2003, to fly over national park and abutting tribal lands. This application process triggers the development of an Air Tour Management Plan (ATMP) by the FAA and NPS for each unit where none exists [http://www.atmp.faa.gov/default.htm]. The purpose of the plans is to mitigate or prevent any adverse impacts of commercial air tours on natural and cultural resources, visitor experiences, and tribal lands. Development of an ATMP requires an environmental analysis under the National Environmental Policy Act of 1969 (NEPA). After applying for operating authority, current air tour operators receive interim permission to continue commercial air tours until the ATMP for the relevant park is completed. The agencies have decided to first develop ATMPs for Haleakala National Park and Hawaii Volcanoes National Park, with the order of other locations to be determined later. About 50 of the nearly 400 NPS units have commercial air tours that would be subject to the new rules.

Finally, the FAA issued a notice of proposed rulemaking on August 8, 2003, that would continue indefinitely existing safety requirements (in Special Federal Aviation Regulation No. 71) for air tours conducted in Hawaii. The regulation initially was issued in 1994 to address safety concerns and air tour accidents in Hawaii. It generally requires a minimum altitude for air tours in Hawaii of 1,500 feet. Air tour operators in Hawaii do not support that minimum altitude and had petitioned the FAA for a reduction to 300 feet to give pilots more discretion. In continuing the 1,500 feet minimum, the FAA noted the success of the rule in reducing air tour accidents in Hawaii and an agency practice of granting operators deviations from the altitude requirement on a case-by-case basis.

## Legislative Activity

H.R. 2115, as passed by the House, sought to prohibit the Administrator of the FAA from restricting commercial operations in the Dragon and Zuni Point corridors of Grand Canyon during certain times. The provision, supported by the air tour industry, would have altered the current curfew to give air tour operators more hours to fly visitors over the Grand Canyon. Some environmentalists and park officials opposed the provision as reducing the amount of quiet in the park. Congress deleted the provision in conference. Conferees instead included bill language directing the Secretary of Transportation to issue a final rule, no later than January 2005, establishing standards for quiet technology that are "reasonably achievable" at Grand Canyon National Park. They also established a mediation process for rulemaking disputes. In adopting this provision, conferees stated that they are "greatly disappointed with the lack of progress" the NPS and FAA have made in managing the impacts on national parks of noise from air tours. They directed the agencies to expeditiously and collaboratively develop ATMPs and determine environmental impacts of air tours.

# RECREATIONAL FEE DEMONSTRATION PROGRAM (BY CAROL HARDY VINCENT)

## Background

Congress is considering whether to extend, amend, or make permanent the Recreational Fee Demonstration Program ("Fee Demo," 16 U.S.C. §460*l* - 6a note). The program allows the four major federal land management agencies — NPS, Bureau of Land Management, Fish and Wildlife Service, and Forest Service — to test the feasibility of recovering some of the costs of operating recreation sites. Each agency can establish any number of fee projects and spend the revenue collected without further appropriation; at least 80% of the funds are to be retained at the collecting site. The NPS typically collects far more revenues than the other three agencies combined, with NPS revenues estimated at $125 million for FY2003. The agencies may spend the money on the repair and maintenance backlog; interpretation; signs; habitat and facility enhancement; resource preservation; maintenance and operation, including the costs of fee collection; and law enforcement. Originally a 3-year trial authorized in FY1996, the program has been extended through FY2004 for fee collection with the revenue available to be spent through FY2007.

The agencies generally favor Fee Demo because it generates substantial revenue and allows discretion in determining fee locations, setting fees, and using the revenues. Critics counter that the fees discriminate against those less able to pay, are a double tax on the recreating public, and, together with other agency fees, confuse the public. The Forest Service's Fee Demo Program has received most of these criticisms.

## Administrative Actions

The Bush Administration supports making the Fee Demo Program permanent, and the FY2004 budget states that the Administration will propose legislation providing permanent fee authority. The Interagency

Recreation Fee Leadership Council, which facilitates coordination and consistency among the agencies on recreation fees, has developed 7 guiding principles for a permanent fee program [http://www.doi.gov/ocl/2002/s2473.htm]. Last Congress the Administration testified in support of establishing an interagency program, a new fee structure to replace entrance and use fees, a single interagency national pass, and site-specific and regional multi-entity passes. The Administration also supports using a large portion of the NPS collections to address the agency's deferred maintenance backlog. In the past, approximately 60% of NPS Fee Demo funds have been allocated to the maintenance backlog, including new construction which may result from deferred maintenance. The NPS has asserted that more analysis is needed to determine whether to shift the current 80/20% split in funds to increase monies for the agency's deferred maintenance needs.

## Legislative Activity

S. 1107 would establish a permanent recreation fee program for the National Park Service only. The Secretary of the Interior is to establish fees based on an analysis of factors including benefits and services to the visitor and comparable fees charged elsewhere. The results of the analysis are to be transmitted to Congress, and no new fees or changes in fees shall take place without at least 12 months notice in the Federal Register. The Secretary may allow discounted or free admission or use. The bill seeks to coordinate fees collected under the Park Service's recreation fee program with fees collected for other purposes, such as the National Park Passport and state agency annual passes. In general, 80% of fees are to be returned to the collecting site, but not less than 90% of fees can be retained by areas with revenue sharing agreements with states. The Secretary determines how the Park Service uses the balance of the collections, and no more than 15% of revenues can be used to administer the program. The Secretary is to report to Congress every three years on the implementation of the program.

The Fee Demo Program would be extended for 2 years under an appropriations bill (H.R. 2691) that passed the House. The bill would extend the program through September 2006 for fee collection and September 2009 for fee expenditures to allow the authorizing committees more time to consider whether to create a permanent program, according to the Appropriations Committee. The House defeated an amendment to limit the extension to National Park units. Also, a GAO report (November 2001) found that agencies in the program could increase innovation in setting and collecting fees, improve program coordination and consistency, and establish performance measures for program managers. The agencies continue to make administrative changes to address concerns with the program.

# THE NATIONAL TRAILS SYSTEM (BY SANDRA L. JOHNSON)

## Background

On October 2, 1968, the National Trails System Act (P.L. 90-543), authorizing the National Trails System (NTS), became law [http://www.nps.gov/nts/]. With the addition of the newly designated Old Spanish National Historic Trail, the federal portion of the trails system consists of 23 national trails (8 scenic trails and 15 historic trails) covering almost 40,000 miles, more than 800 recreation trails, and 2 connecting and side trails. More than three decades since the trails system began, issues remain regarding funding, quality, and quantity of trails.

## Administrative Actions

On June 5, 2003, the Director of the National Park Service, announced the designation by Interior Secretary Gale Norton of 23 National Recreation Trails (NRTs) in 12 states. Also, Ann Veneman, Secretary of Agriculture, designated 4 nonmotorized NRTs on USDA lands. According to Veneman "these designations contribute to President Bush's Healthier US initiative by providing opportunities for the public to exercise in the great outdoors." Each of the 27 newly designated NRTs will receive a certificate of designation and National Recreation Trail markers.

On January 18, 2003, Secretary Norton addressed the official Commencement of the Lewis and Clark Bicentennial at Monticello in Charlottesville, VA. Twenty-one agencies signed a memorandum of understanding to collaborate on the commemoration of the Bicentennial. The federal interagency touring exhibition, named the *Corps of Discovery II: 200 Years to the Future,* launched the three-year (2003-2006) national celebration which will extend from Virginia to the Oregon coast. The National Park Service, under the authority of the Lewis and Clark National Historic Trail, provides design, transportation, support staff, and funding.

The Bicentennial was funded at $12.1 million for FY2003, and $11.8 million is requested for FY2004.

## Legislative Activity

The Senate Energy and Natural Resources Subcommittee on National Parks held a hearing on May 6, 2003 on four national trails bills (S. 324, S. 634, S. 635, and S. 651). S. 324 and S. 651 would amend the NTS Act to clarify federal authority to acquire land from willing sellers for certain trails. S. 324 would give acquisition authority to the Ice Age and the North Country NSTs. S. 651, as passed by the Senate on July 17, 2003, would limit land acquisitions along the Oregon, Mormon Pioneer, Lewis and Clark, Iditarod, Nez Perce National Historic Trails, and Continental Divide National Scenic Trail to an average of not more than one-quarter mile on either side of the trail. The bill would provide federal land managers the authority to acquire land beyond the one-quarter width for the North Country, Ice Age, and Potomac Heritage National Scenic Trails.

On June 16, 2003, the Senate passed S. 635, to direct the Secretary of the Interior to update the feasibility and suitability studies of four trails: the California National Historic Trail, Oregon National Historic Trail, Pony Express National Historic Trail, and Mormon Pioneer National Historic Trail. S. 634, authorizing a study of the feasibility of designating the Trail of the Ancients, was not supported at the hearing by the National Park Service, since "the roads proposed for this trail are highways built by the States to connect the various sites...." The area will be studied for possible designation as a National Heritage Area instead of a trail. Some of the testimony addressed the impact on private property rights and development, including oil and gas drilling, of possible federal restrictions on activities within view of a designated trail.

The several bills introduced in the 108th Congress to designate or study specific trails are shown in the following table. Two additional bills (S. 324 and S. 651) to clarify federal authority for acquiring land for trails are listed in the "Legislation" section below.

| Bill Number | Type | Title | Status |
|---|---|---|---|
| H.R. 461/H.R. 2327/S. 642 | Extend | Lewis and Clark NHT Amendments Act of 2003 | Introduced |
| H.R. 897 | Study | Mississippi River Trail Study Act | Introduced |
| H.R. 1051/ S. 635 | Study Study | Pioneer National Historic Trails Studies Act Pioneer National Historic Trails Studies Act | Introduced Passed Senate; Referred to House Comm. |
| H.R. 1520 | Study | Forks of the Ohio NST Study Act of 2003 | Introduced |
| S. 634 | Study | NHT Study of the Trail of the Ancients | Hearing Held |

# HERITAGE AREAS (BY DAVID WHITEMAN)

## Background

Over the last two decades, Congress has designated 23 National Heritage Areas to recognize and assist areas and protect resources that may not qualify for inclusion in the National Park System. Heritage Areas are collaborative partnerships between the NPS, states, and local communities to conserve, commemorate, and promote distinctive regional landscapes and resources. They have been supported as promoting tourism and community revitalization. Heritage lands remain in state, local government, or private ownership. Property-rights advocates fear that the NPS could exert federal control over non-federal lands by influencing zoning and land use planning in ways that could impede development.

Congress considers measures to study whether to establish heritage areas and bills to designate new heritage areas. Congress also determines which areas will receive funding and specifies the amount of funds. Heritage areas do not receive permanent funding, but are encouraged to become self-sufficient. The Park Service seeks to limit each area to $1 million per year, not to exceed $10 million overall. There is no statute establishing criteria for heritage areas or providing standards for their funding and management, prompting criticism that the process could result in the designation of inappropriate areas or in longterm managerial and financial obligations by the Park Service. There is also a growing concern about the proliferation of bills to create heritage areas. Pending legislation would nearly double their number, increasing the administrative and financial obligations of the NPS. Some of the pending measures would create heritage "corridors," "routes," and "partnerships," which are considered by the NPS to be heritage areas.

There is also growth in the formation of state heritage programs that are not connected with the federal program; 8 states now have heritage programs of their own. A recent White House initiative; "Preserve America,"(E.O. 13287, March 3, 2003) encourages federal government agencies to seek "...partnerships with State and local governments, Indian tribes, and the private sector to promote the preservation of the unique cultural heritage of communities and of the Nation ..." Also, the Alliance of National Heritage Areas (ANHA) [http://www.nationalheritageareas.com], a collaboration of the 23 congressionally-designated National Heritage Areas, provides training to practitioners of heritage development, operates a resources center for heritage areas, and promotes heritage tourism.

## Administrative Actions

The NPS has formed an administrative entity, the Heritage Partnership Program, to advise and assist heritage areas. The agency assists communities in attaining the heritage area designation, and provides a variety of types of assistance to areas once designated — administrative, budget, policy, technical, and public information. It provides limited financial assistance. Further, at congressional request, the NPS prepares studies as to the suitability of designating heritage areas.

## Legislative Activity

H.R. 1427 would establish criteria and mechanisms for designating heritage areas, management standards, and funding support limits. Similar legislation was considered in The 107th Congress, but was not enacted. In recent Congresses, NPS representatives have testified in favor of developing legislation to provide criteria and standards for the establishment, management, and financial assistance of heritage areas. Current bills to designate or study specific areas are shown in table format below.

Congress appropriated $13 million in FY2002 for heritage area studies and management plans, and $14.3 million for FY2003. While the Administration sought to reduce funding to $7.7 million for FY2004, an appropriations bill passed by the House (H.R. 2691) would provide $13.9 million and the companion bill reported by the Senate Committee on Appropriations (S. 1391) would provide $13.6 million. The House appropriations bill also would establish the Blue Ridge National Heritage Area in North Carolina.

| Bill Number | State | Type | Title | Status |
|---|---|---|---|---|
| H.R. 280/S. 180 | OH/IN | Desig. | National Aviation Heritage Area Act | Introduced |
| H.R. 505/S. 211 | NM | Desig. | Northern Rio Grande National Heritage Area Act | Introduced |
| H.R. 524/S. 230 | NJ | Desig. | Crossroads of the American Revolution Nat. Heritage Act | Introduced |
| H.R. 567/S.472 | VA | Study | Northern Neck National Heritage Area Study Act | Introduced |
| H.R. 744/S. 276 | SC | Study | Southern Campaign of the Revolution Heritage Area Study Act | Introduced |
| H.R. 907 | CA | Study | Highway 49, "Golden Chain Highway" National Heritage Corridor Study Act | Introduced |
| H.R. 1069/S. 577 | MA/NH | Desig. | Freedom's Way National Heritage Area Act | Introduced |
| H.R. 1594 | VI | Study | St. Croix National Heritage Area Study Act | Introduced |
| H.R. 1618 | GA | Desig. | Arabia Mountain National Heritage Area Act | Introduced |
| H.R. 1759/S. 941 H.R. 2691 | NC | Desig. | Blue Ridge National Heritage Area Act | Introduced H. Passed |
| H.R. 1798/S. 1056 | CT/MA | Desig. | Upper Housatonic Valley Nat. Heritage Area Act | Introduced |
| H.R. 1862/S. 912 | PA | Desig. | Oil Region National Heritage Area Act | Introduced |
| H.R. 2278/S. 1330 | AK | Desig. | Kenai Mountains-Turnagain Arm Nat. Heritage Corridor Act/Heritage Area Act | Introduced |
| H.R. 2689/S. 1137 | MS | Desig. | Mississippi Gulf Coast National Heritage Area Act | Introduced |
| H.R. 2925 | NC | Study | Northeastern N. Carolina Heritage Area Study Act | Introduced |
| S. 323 | LA | Desig. | Atchafalaya National Heritage Area Act | Introduced |
| S. 840 | NV/UT | Desig. | Great Basin National Heritage Route Act | Introduced |
| S. 916 | UT | Desig. | National Mormon Pioneer Heritage Area Act | Introduced |
| S. 1105 | MO | Study | French Colonial Heritage Nat. Hist. Site Study Act | Introduced |
| S. 1118 | VT/NY | Desig. | Champlain Valley Nat. Heritage Partnership Act | Introduced |

## LEGISLATION

### H.R. 1130 (Holt); S. 965 (Reid)

Requires implementation of the final rule to phase out snowmobile use in Yellowstone and Grand Teton National Parks and John D. Rockefeller, Jr. Memorial Parkway. H.R. 1130 introduced March 6, 2003; referred to Committee on Resources. S. 965 introduced May 1, 2003; referred to Committee on Energy and Natural Resources.

### H.R. 1427 (Hefley)

The National Heritage Areas Policy Act establishes criteria and mechanisms for designating national heritage areas. Introduced March 25, 2003; referred to Committee on Resources.

### H.R. 1517 (Graves)

Amends the Land and Water Conservation Fund to limit the use of funds to maintenance needs of the land management agencies and to require those agencies to reduce backlogged maintenance by certain amounts within 5-year intervals. Introduced March 31, 2003; referred to Committee on Resources and Committee on Agriculture.

### H.R. 1831 (Renzi)

Extends the grace period for personal watercraft use in Glen Canyon National Recreation Area until October 31, 2003. Introduced April 12, 2003; referred to Committee on Resources.

### H.R. 2115 (Young, Don)

Contains a provision directing the Secretary of Transportation to issue a final rule, no later than January 2005, establishing standards for quiet technology that are "reasonably achievable" at Grand Canyon National Park. July 25, 2003, conference report filed.

## S. 324 (Levin)

Amends the National Trails System Act to clarify federal authority for acquiring land from willing sellers for two NSTs. Introduced Feb. 6, 2003; referred to Committee on Energy and Natural Resources. May 6, 2003, Subcommittee hearing held.

## S. 651 (Allard)

The National Trails System Willing Seller Act amends the National Trails System Act to clarify federal authority for acquiring land from willing sellers for four NSTs and five NHTs. July 17, 2003, passed Senate. July 18, 2003, referred to House Resources.

## S. 917 (Murkowski)

Requires that tax revenues from fuel purchased for snowmachine use be used for winter motorized access trails. Introduced April 11, 2003; referred to Committee on Environment and Public Works.

## S. 1107 (Thomas)

Establishes a permanent recreation fee program for the National Park Service. Introduced May 22, 2003; referred to Committee on Energy and Natural Resources.

# CONGRESSIONAL HEARINGS, REPORTS, AND DOCUMENTS

U.S. Congress, House Committee on Resources, *National Heritage Areas Policy Act*, H.Rept. 107-498, 107th Cong., 2nd Sess., June 11, 2002, Washington, DC, 2002.

— Subcommittee on National Parks and Public Lands, *Issues Regarding the New NPS Methodology Used to Evaluate the Achievement of Natural Quiet Restoration Standards in Grand Canyon National Park*, hearing, 106th Cong., 1st Sess., May 25, 1999, Washington, DC, 1999.

U.S. Congress, House Committee on Small Business, *Protecting Small Business and National Parks: The Goals Are Not Mutually Exclusive*, hearing, 107th Cong., 2nd Sess., January 26, 2002, West Yellowstone, MT. At [http://www.house.gov/smbiz/hearings/107th/2002/020126/index.html].

U.S. Congress, Senate Committee on Energy and Natural Resources, *National Discovery Trails Act of 2001*, S.Rept. 107-26, 107th Cong., 1st Sess., June 5, 2001, Washington, DC, 2001.

—— *National Trails System Willing Seller Act*, S.Rept. 107-276, 107th Cong., 2nd Sess., September 12, 2002, Washington, DC, 2002.

—— *Omnibus National Heritage Area Act of 2002*, S.Rept. 107-286, 107th Cong., 2nd Sess., September 17, 2002, Washington, DC, 2002.

—— Subcommittee on National Parks, Historic Preservation, and Recreation, *Snowmobile Activities in the National Park System and Miscellaneous National Heritage Bills*, hearing, 106th Cong., 2nd Sess., May 18-25, 2000, Washington, DC, 2000.

*Chapter 2*

# NATIONAL PARK SYSTEM: ESTABLISHING NEW UNITS*

## *Carol Hardy Vincent*

## INTODRODUCTION

The National Park Service includes 378 diverse units administered by
the National Park Service (NPS) of the Department of the Interior (DOI).
The resources of the those units are to be preserved unimpaired for future
generations. units generally are added to the National Park System by an act
of Congress, although the President may proclaim national monuments on
federal land for inclusion in the system. Before inacting a law to add a unit,
Congress might first enact a law requiring the NPS to study a prospective
area, typically to assess its national significance and other factors. The
Secretary of the Interior is required to prepare annually for Congress a list of
areas recommended for study, as well as certain lists of areas previously
studied. Significant areas also can be preserved outside the National Park
System through programs managed or supported by NPS.

The National Park System contains 378 units throughout the nation.
They are administered by the National Park Service of the Department of the
Interior. The National Park System encompasses 83.4 million acres of land -
77.4 million acres federally owned and 6.0 million acres of private and other

* Excerpted from CRS Report RS20158. April 16, 1999.

public land (e.g. state land) within NPS unit boundaries. Units range in size from less than one acre to more than 13 million acres. Nearly two-thirds of the total acreage is in Alaska.

In 1872, Congress created Yellowstone, the world's first national park. Subsequently, the nation slowly developed a system of national parks. While some new areas were administered by DOI, others were managed by different agencies. A 1916 law created NPS within DOI to protect existing and future parks, monuments, and other areas. It charged NPS with promoting and regulating the use of those areas both to conserve them and to provide for their enjoyment by the public. A 1933 executive order furthered the development of a national system by transferring dozens of sites to NPS from other agencies. The General Authorities Act of 1970 made explicit that all areas managed by NPS were part of a single system, and gave all units of the system equal standing with regard to resource protection. However, statutes authorizing particular units sometimes provide additional management direction for those units.

Today, there are more than 20 different types of designations for units of the National Park System, reflecting the diversity of the areas. There are 54 units called national parks, the so-called "crown jewels" of the system. Other commonly used titles include national historic sites (77), national monuments (73), national historical parks (38), national memorials (28), national recreation areas (19), and national preserves (16). Some classifications are unique to NPS, while others, such as national recreation areas and national trails, also are used by other land management agencies. In recent years, Congress and NPS have attempted to simplify and standardize classifications.[1]

Units of the system generally are managed to preserve resources in their natural or historical conditions for the benefit of future generations. Thus, hunting, mining, and other consumptive resource uses generally are not allowed. However, in the laws creating units, Congress sometimes has specified that some of those uses are allowed.

---

[1] A brief definition for each classification, together with a description of each unit of the system, is included in U.S. Dept. of the Interior, National Park Service, Office of Public Affairs and the Division of Publications, *The National Parks: Index 1997-1999*, (Washington: GPO, 1997).

# CREATING MONUMENTS BY PRESIDENTIAL PROCLAMATION

Additions to the National Park System usually are made by act of Congress. However, national monuments may be added to the system by presidential proclamation, as well as by act of Congress. The Antiquities Act of 1906 (16 U.S.C. 431 et seq.) authorizes the President to create national monuments on federal land that contains historic landmarks, historic and prehistoric structures, or other objects of historic or scientific interest.[2] The President is to reserve "the smallest area compatible with the proper care and management" of the protected objects.

More than 100 monuments have been proclaimed by many Presidents since 1906. Congress has subsequently converted many of them, such as the Grand Canyon, to national parks. National monuments typically are managed by NPS. A prominent exception is the Grand Staircase-Escalante National Monument in Utah, which is managed by the Bureau of Land Management under the 1996 presidential proclamation.

# ADDING UNITS BY PUBLIC LAW

Except for proclaimed monuments, National Park System units are created by act of Congress. An act may explain the unit's purpose; set its boundaries; provide specific directions for land acquisition, planning, management, and operations; and authorize appropriations for acquisition and development. Bills to create units are within the jurisdiction of the House Committee on Resources and the Senate Committee on Energy and Natural Resources, with appropriations typically contained in Department of the Interior and Related Agencies Appropriations Acts.

In recent years, Congress sometimes has enacted free-standing legislation to add units to the National Park System. Congress also has authorized units as part of omnibus parks and recreation laws containing dozens of recreation-related measures. Measures sometimes are packaged to facilitate broad evaluation of an issue and to expedite consideration. Legislation creating a new unit may be preceded by legislation to authorize an NPS study of the area, as described below.

---

[2] Extensions or establishment of monuments in Wyoming require the authorization of Congress (16 U.S.C. 431a), and withdrawals in Alaska exceeding 5,000 acres are subject to congressional approval (16 U.S.C. 3213).

Provisions of law, together with NPS policies, affect Congress's consideration of measures to create units of the National Park System.[3] In 1998, Congress amended existing law pertaining to the creation of new units (P.L. 105-391) to standardize procedures, improve the information about potential additions, prioritize areas, focus attention on outstanding areas, and ensure congressional support for area studies. Current law charges the Secretary of the Interior with investigating, studying, and monitoring nationally significant areas with potential for inclusion in the system. In the past, the National Park System Advisory Board, composed of private citizens, advised the Secretary on possible additions to, and policies for management of, the system. In practice, NPS performs the functions assigned to the Secretary.

## RECOMMENDING AREAS FOR STUDY

The Secretary of the Interior is required by law to submit annually to Congress a list of areas recommended for study for potential inclusion in the National Park System. Candidates for study are identified by diverse sources, such as local "grassroots" preservation interests, elected officials, and professional evaluations. The Secretary's annual list for Congress of damaged or threatened areas on the Registry of Natural Landmarks and the National Register of Historic Places also has been used to identify study sites. NPS screens candidates, in some cases conducting a brief site visit or a more detailed reconnaissance survey to assess an area. NPS ranks areas that pass the initial screening, and the highest priority areas are recommended to Congress for study Any detailed study for inclusion in the system requires congressional authorization.

Under 16 U.S.C. la-S, NPS must consider three issues in assessing whether to study particular areas: whether an area is nationally significant, and would be a suitable and feasible addition to the National Park System; whether an area represents or includes themes, sites, or resources "not adequately" represented in the system; and requests for studies in the form of public petitions and congressional resolutions (the "popular demand" factor).

---

[3] See 16 U.S.C. la-5 for provisions of law, and the NPS website ( http://www.nps.gov/legacy/ criteria.html ) for agency policies and criteria.

# PREPARING AREA STUDIES

Under the 1998 statute (P.L. 105-391), any actual study requires "specific authorization of an Act of Congress." However, NPS may conduct preliminary activities, such as a resource assessment, provided that the activity does not cost more than $25,000. In the past, studies were directed by authorization and appropriations laws and prepared at the initiative of NPS, individual Members of Congress, and other entities. The 1998 statute sought to eliminate these separate sources for initiating studies, on the grounds that in some years funding was insufficient to cover all studies, and ongoing studies sometimes were not completed because funds were earmarked for other studies. Nevertheless, the new law does not appear to explicitly require a preliminary study before Congress adds a unit to the system.

After funds are made available, NPS must complete a study within 3 fiscal years. Studies are to include public involvement, with at least one public meeting held in the local area, and reasonable efforts to notify affected state and local governments and landowners. Studies also are to comply with the National Environmental Policy Act of 1969 (NEPA), which requires an assessment of the potential impact of the proposed action on the human environment Criteria for Studies. In preparing studies, when directed by Congress, NPS must consider certain factors established in law to promote the consistency and professionalism of the studies. The factors elaborate on criteria long included in NPS policies. NPS is directed to assess whether an area contains natural or cultural resources that are nationally significant, constitutes one of the most important examples of a type of resource, and presents a suitable and feasible addition to the system.

The NPS has developed criteria for determining national significance, suitability, and feasibility. An area will be regarded as nationally significant if it is an outstanding example of a resource; exceptionally illustrates or interprets our nation's natural or cultural themes; provides extraordinary opportunities for recreation, public use, or scientific study; and contains a true, accurate, and relatively unspoiled resource.[4]

In the past, NPS has considered recreational areas, as well as natural and cultural ones, in evaluating national significance, and has developed examples of each kind. (The Advisory Board has recommended that recreation alone not be used to evaluate national significance.) A nationally

---

[4] Information in this section on criteria is derived primarily from the NPS website: (http://www.nps.gov/legacy/criteria.html visited January 6, 1999).

significant natural area might be a refuge that is critical for the survival of a species. Cultural areas might include districts, sites, structures, or objects of exceptional quality in interpreting our nation's heritage, such as those with distinctive architectural types. Cultural entities generally exclude cemeteries, birth places, graves, religious properties, relocated structures, reconstructed buildings, and properties of significance within the past 50 years. A qualifying recreational area might have a natural or cultural aspect that offers a unique setting for varied types of recreation.

NPS views an area as suitable if it portrays a theme or resource insufficiently included in the system, unless a similar area is managed for public use by another agency. An area is feasible to add if it is large enough, configured so as to allow long-term protection and public use, and affordable to manage. Other important issues involve ownership of the land and the cost of acquiring it, access, threats to resources, and staff or development requirements. For instance, privately owned land that the owner is unwilling to sell, or that would be expensive to acquire, might not be viewed as feasible.

Under 16 U.S.C. la-5, NPS studies must evaluate other factors about an area, including the rarity and integrity of the resources; resource threats; whether similar resources already are protected; the probable costs of its acquisition, development, and operation; the socioeconomic effects of adding it; the interpretive and educational uses; the potential for public use; the extent of public, including local, support; and whether the configuration ensures long-term protection and use.

## Other Management Options

In studying an area, NPS must consider whether NPS management or alternative protection is appropriate. Options noted in NPS management policies include administration by other federal agencies, state or local governments, Native American authorities, and the private sector. Consideration may be given to other forms of aid, such as technical or financial; other designations, including national trail or national historic landmark; and cooperative management between NPS and another agency. NPS generally will not recommend adding an area to the National Park System if another arrangement already provides, or could provide for, sufficient protection and public use. The study must identify the best alternative(s) for protecting resources and allowing public enjoyment. Each study sent to Congress must be accompanied by a letter from the Secretary that identifies the preferred management option for the area, so as to minimize uncertainty about NPS's position.

## LISTS OF AREAS PREVIOUSLY STUDIED

The NPS also must submit to Congress an annual list of areas previously studied that contain primarily historical resources, and a similar list of areas with natural resources. Areas are to be ranked in order of priority for potential addition to the National Park System, based upon the expanded criteria for determining the rankings contained in law. In developing the lists, the Secretary of the Interior is required to consider not only threats to resource values and cost escalation factors, but the issues considered when preparing the initial studies. Areas on the lists must be supported by accurate and current data.

## ISSUES

The addition of units to the National Park System sometimes has been controversial. Some discourage adding units, arguing that the system is "mature" or "complete," while others assert that the system should evolve and grow to reflect current events, new information, and reinterpretations. Differences exist on the relative importance of including areas reflecting our natural, cultural, and social history. The adequacy of standards and procedures for assuring that the most outstanding areas are included in the system also has been a subject of much debate. Critics contend that the system has been weakened by including inappropriate areas, especially where authoritative information was unavailable, incomplete, or disregarded in favor of political considerations. Others counter that there will always be disagreement over the worth of areas, and that recently added areas have been held to the same high standards as older units. How to properly maintain existing and new units given limited resources also has been at issue. Some have cited existing NPS fiscal and staffing constraints in arguing against creating new units, particularly without a commensurate increase in NPS funds; supporters of new units have charged that the older units are the most costly. Another issue has been whether particular resources are better protected outside the National Park System, and how to secure the best alternative protection.

# ALTERNATIVES TO INCLUSION
# IN THE NATIONAL PARK SYSTEM

It is generally regarded as difficult to meet the criteria and to secure congressional support and funding for expanding the National Park System. Although there may be hundreds or thousands of related inquiries to Congress and the NPS, usually no more than a handful of new units are created each Congress.

Significant areas are preserved outside the National Park System. Some of these are protected with recognition or assistance by the NPS. Certain areas that receive technical or financial aid from the NPS, but are neither federally owned nor directly administered by the NPS, have been classified by the NPS as affiliated areas. In the past, the affiliated areas have been given special recognition by Congress, and have included an array of properties primarily recognized for cultural or commemorative worth. Affiliated areas have been created by act of Congress and by designation of the Secretary of the Interior.

National Heritage Areas, a designation recently established by Congress, contain land and properties that reflect the history of their people. They consist mainly of private properties and may include natural, scenic, historic, cultural, or recreation resources. Conservation, interpretation, and other activities are handled by partnerships among federal, state, and local governments and nonprofit organizations, and for each area Congress has recognized a "management entity" to coordinate efforts. The NPS supports these efforts through technical and financial assistance, usually for a temporary period. Supporters of Heritage Areas have asserted that they reduce pressure to add new, costly, and possibly inappropriate areas to the National Park System, while opponents have feared that they could be used to extend federal control over nonfederal land. Differences also have existed over whether to create a comprehensive heritage program containing priorities and standards for establishing Heritage Areas.

Some programs give places honorary recognition. Cultural resources may be listed by the NPS in the National Register of Historic Places, as meriting preservation and special consideration in planning for federal or federally assisted projects. The Secretary of the Interior may designate natural areas as national natural landmarks, and cultural areas as national historic landmarks. National parks, monuments, and other areas of international worth may, at the request of the United States, be recognized by the United Nations as world heritage sites or biosphere reserves. The

Congress, or the Secretary of the Interior, may designate rivers as components of the National Wild and Scenic Rivers System, and trails as part of the National Trails System.

NPS experts and programs support local and state governments in protecting resources. The NPS may provide grants for projects (including acquisition and development of recreational facilities), and technical assistance (for conserving rivers, trails, natural areas, and cultural resources). In addition to this broad range of NPS programs, a variety of resources are protected by the private sector, state and local governments, and other federal agencies.

*Chapter 3*

# THE NATIONAL TRAILS SYSTEM: AN OVERVIEW[*]

## *Sandra L. Johnson*

## INTRODUCTION

The National Trails System Act, P.L. 90-543, became law October 2, 1968. The Act and its subsequent amendments authorized a national system of trails and defined four categories of national trails. Since the designation of the Appalachian and Pacific Crest National Scenic Trails as the first two components, the System has grown to include 20 national trails. Now, 30 years after its inception, issues ret remain regarding funding, quality and quantity of trails, new trail categories, and nationwide promotion to make Americans more aware of the System. This report will be updated as legislative actions occur.

The National Trails System (NTS) was created in 1968 by the National Trails System Act (NTSA).[1] The Act established the Appalachian and Pacific Crest National Scenic Trails and authorized a national system of trails to provide additional outdoor recreation opportunities and to promote the preservation of access to the outdoor areas and historic resources of the nation. The National Trails System includes four classes of trails:

---

[*] Excerpted from CRS Report 98-981 ENR.
[1] Act of Oct 2, 1968; PL. 90-543, 82 Stat. 919, 16 U.S.C. §§ 1241-51.

- **National Scenic Trails (NST)** provide outdoor recreation and the conservation and enjoyment of significant scenic, historic, natural, or cultural qualities;
- **National Historic Trails (NHT)** follow travel routes of national historic significance;
- **National Recreation Trails (NRT)** are in, or reasonably accessible to, urban areas on federal, state, or private lands; and
- **Connecting or Side Trails** provide access to or among the other classes of trails.

## BACKGROUND

During the early history of the United States, trails served as routes for commerce and migration. Since the early 20th Century, trails have been constructed to provide access to scenic terrain. In 1921, the concept of the first interstate recreational trail, now known as the Appalachian National Scenic Trail, was introduced. In 1945, legislation to establish a "national system of foot trails," an amendment to a highway funding bill, was considered by not reported by committee.[2]

As population expanded in the 1950s, an eager nation sought better opportunities to enjoy the outdoors.[3] In 1958, Congress established and directed the Outdoor Recreation Resources Review Commission (ORRRC) to make a nationwide study of outdoor national recreation needs. A 1960 survey conducted for the ORRRC indicated that 90% of all Americans participated in some form of outdoor recreation and that walking for pleasure ranked second among all recreation activities.[4] On February 8, 1965, President Lyndon B. Johnson, in his message to Congress on "Natural Beauty," called for the Nation "to copy the great Appalachian Trail in all parts of our country, and make full use of rights-of-way and other public paths."[5] Just 3 years later, Congress heeded the message by enacting the National Trails System Act.

The National Trails System began in 1968 with only two scenic trails. One was the Appalachian National Scenic Trail, stretching 2,160 miles from

---

[2] Donald D. Jackson, "The Long Way 'Round," *Wilderness* vol. 51, no. 181 (summer, 1988): 19-20.
[3] Outdoor Recreation Resources Review Commission. *Outdoor Recreation for America.* Washington, D.C. January 1962. p.34.
[4] *Ibid.*, p 1.
[5] Congressional Record, vol. 3, Feb. 8, 1965), p. 2087.

Mount Katahdin, Maine, to Springer Mountain, Georgia. The second was the Pacific Crest National Scenic Trail, covering 2,665 miles from Canada to Mexico along the mountains of Washington, Oregon, and California. The System was expanded a decade later when the National Parks and Recreation Act of 1978 designated four historic trails with more than 9,000 miles, and another scenic trail, along the Continental Divide, with 3,100 miles. Today, the federal portion of the System consists of 20 national trails (8 scenic trails, 12 historic trails) covering almost 40,000 miles and listed in table 1. In addition, the Act has authorized 1,000 rails-to-trails conversions, more than 800 national recreation trails, and 2 connecting or side trails.

## DESIGNATION

As defined in the National Trails System Act, NSTs and NHTs are long distance trails and are designated as national trails by Acts of Congress. NRTs and connecting and side trails may be designated by the Secretaries of the Interior and Agriculture with the consent of the federal agency, state, or political subdivision over the lands involved. Of the 39 feasibility studies requested since 1968, 5 NSTs and 12 NUTs have been designated.

The Secretaries are permitted to acquire lands or interest in lands for the National Trails System by written cooperative agreements, through donations, by purchase with donated or appropriated funds, by exchange, and, within limited authority, by condemnation. The Secretaries are directed to cooperate with and encourage states to administer non-federal trail lands through cooperative agreements with landowners and private organizations for the rights-of-way or through states or local governments acquiring such lands or interests.

**Table 1.** Federal Components of the National Trail System

| Year | Trail | Public Law |
|------|-------|-----------|
| 1968 | Appalachian NST | P.L. 90-543 |
| 1968 | Pacific Crest NST | P.L. 90-543 |
| 1978 | Continental Divide NST | P.L. 95-25 |
| 1978 | Oregon NHT | P.L. 95-25 |
| 1978 | Mormon Pioneer NHT | P.L. 95-25 |
| 1978 | Iditarod NHT | P.L. 9525 |
| 1978 | Lewis and Clark NHT | P.L. 95-25 |
| 1980 | North Country NST | P.L. 96-199 |
| 1980 | Overmountain Victory NHT | P.L. 96-344 |
| 1980 | Ice Age NST | P.L. 96-370 |
| 1983 | Florida NST | P.L. 98-11 |
| 1983 | Potomac Heritage NST | P.L. 98-11 |
| 1983 | Natchez Trace NST | P.L. 98-11 |
| 1986 | Nez Perce (Nee-Me-Poo) NHT | P.L. 99-445 |
| 1987 | Santa Fe NHT | P.L. 100-35 |
| 1987 | Trail of Tears NHT | P.L. 100-192 |
| 1990 | Juan Bautistade Anza NHT | P.L. 101-365 |
| 1992 | California NHT | P.L. 102-328 |
| 1992 | Pony Express NHT | P.L. 102-328 |
| 1996 | Selma to Montgomery NHT | P.L. 104-333 |

## ORGANIZATION AND MANAGEMENT

Each national trail is administered by either the Secretary of the Interior or the Secretary of Agriculture under the authority of the National Trails System Act. The National Park Service administers 15 of the 20 trails in the NTS; the Forest Service administers 4 trails; and Bureau of Land Management administers one. The Secretaries are to administer the federal lands, working cooperatively with agencies managing lands not under their jurisdiction. Management responsibilities vary for the type of trail.

## National Scenic Trails

NSTs provide recreation, conservation and enjoyment of significant scenic, historic, natural, or cultural qualities. The use of motorized vehicles on these long-distance trails is generally prohibited, except for the Continental Divide National Scenic Trail which allows: (1) access for emergencies; (2) reasonable access for adjacent landowners (including timber rights); and (3) landowner use on private lands in the right of way, in accordance with regulations established by the administering Secretary.

## National Historic Trails

These trails follow travel routes of national historical significance. To qualify for designation as a NHT, the proposed trail must meet all of the following criteria: (1) the route must have documented historical significance as a result of its use and location; (2) there must be evidence of a trail's national significance with respect to American history; and (3) the trail must have significant potential for public recreational use or historical interest. These trails do not have to be continuous, and can include land and water segments, marked highways paralleling the route, and sites that together form a chain or network along the historic route.[6]

## National Recreation Trails

The Forest Service administers national recreation trails within national forests, while the National Park Service is responsible for the overall administration of the national recreation trails program on all other lands, including coordination of non-federal trails. NRTs are existing trails in or reasonably accessible to urban areas, recognized by the federal government as contributing to the Trails System and are managed by public and private agencies at the local, state and national levels.[7] There are NRTs which provide recreation opportunities for the handicapped, hikers, bicyclists, cross country skiers, and horseback riders.

---

[6] http://www.nps.gov/planning/trails/newsletter/news1.htm.
[7] http://www.nps.gov/pub_aff/naltrail.htm.

## Connecting and Side Trails

These trails provide public access to nationally designated trails or connections between such trails, They are administered by the Secretary of the Interior, except that the Secretary of Agriculture administers those trails located on national forest lands.

# ISSUES

## Funding

The level of funding continues to be the biggest trail issue. With the exception of the Appalachian and the Pacific Crest NSTs, the National Trails System Act does not provide for sustained finding of designated trails operations, maintenance and development, nor does the Act authorize dedicated finds for land acquisition.

On June 9, 1998, President Clinton signed into law P.L. 105-178, the Transportation Equity Act for the 21st Century (TEA-21). TEA-21 is the 6-year reauthorization of the Intermodal Surface Transportation Efficiency of 1991 (ISTEA).[8] ISTEA included the National Recreational Trails Fund Act (16 U.S.C. §§1261-1262, which is separate from the National Trails System Act) and established the National Recreational Trails Funding Program (Recreational Trails Program). The Recreational Trails Program provides funds to the states to develop and maintain recreational trails and trail-related facilities for both non-motorized and motorized recreational trail uses. Trail uses include bicycling, hiking, in-line skating, cross-country skiing, snownmobiling, off-road motorcycling, all-terrain vehicle riding, four-wheel driving, or using other off-road motorized vehicles.

## Extent and Nature of System

Another issue is the appropriate number of trails. Some ask, "How many national trails are enough?" If the six new long-distance trails considered in the 105th Congress had been added to the National Trails System, the System would extend to every state, except Rhode Island. According to some observers, one of the weaknesses in the NTS, is that "a poor definition exists of which kinds of trails should be part of the System (except for NHT criteria)." While it is relatively easy to add new trails to the System, it has proven more difficult to provide them with adequate staffing and partnership resources.

The 105th Congress considered, but did not enact, legislation to (1) amend the National Trails System by adding "National Discovery Trails" as a new category of long-distance trails (S. 1069, passed Senate), and (2) designate the "American Discovery Trail" (ADT) as the nation's first coast-to-coast National Discovery Trail (H.R. 588). Some have questioned the need for a new category of trails. The ADT, as proposed, would connect several national scenic, historic, and recreation trails, as well as many other local and regional trails.

Finally, some trails supporters have advocated a nationwide promotion to inform the public about the National Trails System. They assert that most Americans are unaware of the Trails System and the breathtaking scenes and journeys into the past which can be experienced along the national scenic and historic trails. However, a significant increase in the number of trails users could overwhelm present staffing and resources.

---

[8] P.L. 102-240.

*Chapter 4*

# STATE OPERATION OF NATIONAL PARKS DURING GOVERNMENT BUDGETARY SHUTDOWNS?[*]

## *David Whiteman*

## INTRODUCTION

National Park System-wide closures resulting from recent government budgetary shutdowns provoked intense complaints, from would-be visitors, and, particularly from financially affected local businesses that lost significant holiday-season business. Legislation to allow State employees to temporarily operate units of the national parks during periods of government budgetary shutdown is being considered by the Congress. The following report examines some of the issues involved.

## DISCUSSION

The budget for the National Park Service (NPS) is included in the annual Interior Department appropriations bill. Because of controversies unrelated to the NPS, the FY1996 DOI appropriations bill (H.R. 1977) was

---

[*] Excerpted from CRS Report 96-105 ENR. February 1, 1996.

not completed before the beginning of the fiscal year. A temporary funding measure was passed to keep the government functioning while Congress continued its struggle to resolve the funding impasse. The House recommitted the conference report on H.R. 1977 to the conference committee twice before the bill was finally passed on December 12, 1995. However, the President vetoed the bill on December 18, and the House failed to override the veto on January 4.

When the initial temporary funding measure expired November 14, 1995, the NPS, along with many other government agencies, was forced to curtail operations. The NPS furloughed most of its employees and closed to the public all of its 369 units. Some NPS staff were designated "essential" to remain in "caretaker status" to protect park assets. Congress and the White House reopened the parks briefly November 20 when they enacted another temporary funding measure in effect until December 15. When that deadline expired without resolution, the NPS was again obligated to close the system, this time for 21 days. Before recessing in early January, Congress approved funding for several particular programs, including the National Park System through September 30, 1996 (the end of the fiscal year). However, activities other than for visitor services have only been funded through January 26.

Park closures during the government shutdown generated substantial public complaint both from inconvenienced and disappointed would-be visitors and especially from financially affected local businesses and communities whose primary customer base are visitors to nearby park units. What was particularly upsetting to these businesses was that while furloughed Federal employees were eventually paid for their time off, even though they could not work, many business people and their employees lost significant holiday-season business that could not be recovered.

During the relatively brief November shutdown, Arizona Governor Fife Symington offered to provide State employees to keep Grand Canyon National Park operating. The NPS declined the offer, saying that existing law would not permit such an abrogation of Federal responsibility. On November 20, immediately following the end of the November shutdown, Representative Don Young, Chairman of the House Committee on Resources, introduced H.R. 2677, to "require the Secretary of the Interior to accept State donations of employee services" to operate any units of the National Park System or the National Wildlife Refuge System, but only during a period of "Government budgetary shutdown," and only if a State volunteered to manage a park or refuge unit located within the State's boundaries.

Members of the Arizona congressional delegation also introduced bills (H.R. 2732 and S. 1451) that would "allow agreements between the Secretary and a State" to operate the national parks in that State with State employees during any period when the agency is unable to maintain normal park operations, e.g., during government shutdowns.

The second partial government shutdown (some spending bills had been enacted) ended after 21 days, with another temporary solution. Many Federal programs have been funded with short-term appropriations (continuing resolutions) set to expire March 15. However, funding for NPS (and other agency) "projects and activities necessary to accommodate visitors and to provide for visitor services" (and various other specified programs) was provided through the end of FY1996 at the lowest of (1) FY1995 appropriations, (2) FY1996 appropriations as passed the House, or (3) FY1996 appropriations as passed the Senate, in §101(a) of P.L. 104-92. Because H.R. 2677 would apply only during a period of government budgetary shutdowns, the relief that H.R. 2677 seeks to provide may have limited, if any, impact on the operation of the NPS during this fiscal year. Such a measure could affect the Parks in the future, however, and Congress may continue to consider the initiative.

A hearing was held on H.R. 2677 on December 8, 1995, before the House Committee on Resources, in anticipation of the second budgetary shutdown after December 15. During the hearings, Representative Bruce Vento, former chairman of the subcommittee with oversight responsibility for the National Park System, questioned the ability of the State of Arizona to administer Grand Canyon National Park. He suggested that the State may not have enough qualified people to manage the park, pointing out that Arizona employs 200 people to operate 22 State parks and that the NPS employs 400 people to operate Grand Canyon alone.

Arizona Governor Symington testified that the Grand Canyon National Park is vital to the economy of his State, citing that the park "generates about $12.5 million annually in sales tax revenues for the State." Park-related tourism is considered the economic lifeblood of a number of communities in proximity to the Grand Canyon. He responded to Mr. Vento's point by asserting that he would also assign State National Guard troops to security and traffic control duties.

George Frampton, Assistant Secretary of the Interior for Fish and Wildlife and Parks, testified that the Administration opposes the legislation because of concerns regarding liability, costs and safety. As to park management in general, he stated that:

Since the bill provides no restrictions on the kinds of functions that State personnel would perform, there is a possibility that compatibility determinations on new public uses and other decisions requiring highly specialized training would be made during a shutdown by State employees who are not familiar with the requirements for such decisions.

H.R. 2677 was brought up for a floor vote in the House on December 12, under a suspension of rules. It failed to attain the required two-thirds' majority (254-156). The legislation could be brought up again under another rule or attached to another legislative vehicle.

Partly underlying the debate on H.R. 2677 are intense and contentious views concerning the management of public lands and the reported desire of some western Republicans to gain, or exert, control over portions of public lands. This struggle has had a number of significant manifestations in the current Congress and legislation has been introduced to allow States to acquire the BLM lands within their borders (H.R. 2032 and S. 1031) and to authorize the Secretary of the Interior to allow the State of South Dakota to operate the three NPS units in the State for 10 years, on a trial basis (S. 1185).

During the December 8 hearings, the Arizona Governor was asked about the idea of a permanent transfer of management responsibility for Grand Canyon National Park to his State, to which the Governor responded: "I like that idea." Such statements have raised some public and Administration concerns that the real intent of H.R. 2677 might be to "prove" that the States can effectively administer these lands, and thus further efforts to transfer Federal lands to State control.

Another alternative is to operate NPS units with Federal personnel and nonfederal funds. During the second 21-day shutdown, the Federal Government agreed to the use of both State and private funds to keep parts of some NPS units operating, creating a precedent for possible future cooperation. These cooperative measures included the following:

- **New Mexico** used funds from a State-private alliance to keep open parts of its largest Federal tourist attraction, Carlsbad Caverns National Park.
- **Arizona** used a special State parks appropriation to pay NPS ranger salaries to keep the Grand Canyon partly open. Arizona's State money was reportedly running out and the Governor had appealed for private donations when the government shutdown ended.

- The City of **Philadelphia** reached an agreement with the Interior Department to use city funds to reopen the Liberty Bell, Congress Hall, and Independence Hall.
- A **South Dakota** rancher paid to keep the lights on the faces on Mount Rushmore at night. A Maryland based bank that uses a Mount Rushmore logo, was later scheduled to takeover payment of the light bill.

National parks are not permitted under current law to use revenue generated at a particular unit to fund operation of that unit. Some of the larger and more popular parks generate significant funds from daily operations. Instead, revenues are deposited in the General Treasury and the Congress appropriates monies to fund national park operations. As long as the annual appropriations for the Interior Department are not enacted, the NPS remains financially restricted. Because of the popularity national parks have with the public some of the current funding mechanisms may be reexamined in the new session of Congress.

*Chapter 5*

# NEW WORLD GOLD MINE AND YELLOWSTONE NATIONAL PARK*

## *Marc Humphries*

### INTRODUCTION

Crown Butte Mines, Inc. wants to develop its New World gold mine deposit located near Yellowstone National Park. The proposed mine is located almost entirely on private property about 3 miles east of the northeast corner of Yellowstone National Park and next to the Absaroka-Beartooth Wilderness area. The New World Mine Project would mine an estimated 1,800 tons of gold/silver/copper ore per day (500,000 tons annually), valued at an estimated $800 million over a 10-15 year period. The project would include an underground mine, an ore processing mill, a tailings pond, a waste rock storage site, access roads, a work camp and transmission lines. A draft environmental impact statement (EIS), required under both NEPA and the Montana Environmental Policy Act, is in the final months of a three-year preparation.

The project has stirred controversy because of its possible environmental impacts. Environmental groups oppose the project because of the potential for damage to water, recreational assets and wildlife in the area, and in particular, to Yellowstone Park itself. Crown Butte maintains it would

---

* Excerpted from CRS Report 96-669 ENR.

employ "state-of-the-art" technology to contain waste in a proposed 106-acre tailings pond. Opponents of the project fear that the tailings pond may fail in the future due to earthquakes, avalanches or other events, leading to acid mine drainage. Several permits from the federal and state level are required to operate the mine and mill. The issuing agencies could approve the mine plan, approve the plan with stipulations, or deny the permit. Without the necessary permits, mine development could not go forward.

Environmentalists have received support from two highly visible events. In July 1995, the President called for a moratorium on mine patents and new claims on federal lands in the area around the mine site. In December 1995, the United Nations World Heritage Committee declared the Yellowstone National Park "in danger" because of the New World mine proposal, and other activities in the area. In the 104th Congress, a Senate proposal (S. 1737) would permanently withdraw from location under the Mining Law 19,000 acres, and affect 5,000 additional acres of federal lands near the Crown Butte mine site. A House bill (H.R. 1846) would withdraw lands upstream from the Park. None of these measures would affect the New World Mine directly, but might affect the economics of the project by precluding future expansion.

## BACKGROUND

The area around Henderson Mountain known as the New World Mining District has been mined for over one hundred years, primarily for gold, silver and copper. The Mining District consists of 130 patented mining claims (2,600 acres). Because of its rich geology, the District has been excluded from wilderness designation even though it is surrounded by wilderness areas and is located only about 3 miles east of the northeast corner of Yellowstone National Park.[1] Portions of the mining district were patented under the General Mining Law of 1872, became private property and are now leased by the owners to Crown Butte Mines, Inc. Some sites, previously overlooked or regarded as uneconomic, are viewed by Crown Butte as having great economic potential. Crown Butte submitted its operating plan for a hardrock mine permit to the Montana State Department of Lands November 15, 1990.

The proximity of the Crown Butte site to Yellowstone National Park has generated opposition to the project. The project is strongly opposed by

---

[1] This information was obtained from the company information package: Crown Butte Mines, Inc., New World Project.

environmental groups because of the potential damage that could occur to the water, recreational assets and wildlife habitats in and around Yellowstone National Park in the event of an accident or the improper treatment of waste.

## Yellowstone National Park

Yellowstone National Park was established by Act of Congress in March 1872 to preserve certain lands from development. It encompasses more than 2 million acres primarily in Wyoming but also in Montana and Idaho. The Park contains a diverse wildlife population, high plateaus, geysers, waterfalls, lakes, and the headwaters for a number of rivers, all of which provide scenic and recreation opportunities for millions of visitors each year.

The area was withdrawn from settlement or sale (including mining activity) and set aside as a "pleasuring ground" for the enjoyment of the people. Later laws were enacted to create the U.S. National Park System and place some public lands off limits to the Mining Law. Other federal laws permitted disposal of lands to the private sector. At issue, in part, is whether Yellowstone National Park and the Absaroka-Beartooth Wilderness would be in danger from acid mine drainage and whether wildlife habitats and wetlands would be destroyed if the Crown Butte project proceeds.

## Federal/State Decisions

Decisions made at the federal and state levels will determine whether the mine plan will go forward. The State of Montana issues the permits necessary to operate a mine. U.S. Forest Service approval is necessary to use Forest Service lands in the project. Legislative and executive proposals (e.g. H.R. 1846, S. 1737) that would withdraw acreage from the Mining Law of 1872, would restrict expansion of the mine. The analysis in the environmental impact statement is expected to be a major factor in federal and state decisions on the mine plan.

Public pressure is likely to come from both the proponents and opponents of the mine plan. Opponents of mine development called upon the United Nations World Heritage Committee to evaluate the potential dangers to Yellowstone that could occur from the New World Mine Proposal. Mine proponents claim that the United Nations input interferes with the EIS process and is unnecessary.

## THE CROWN BUTTE PLAN

Crown Butte Mines, Inc., an U.S. subsidiary of Canadian-owned Noranda, Inc.[2] has either leases or claims to about 2,600 acres of private and public lands. The actual mine sites are leased from private owners by Crown Butte. About 85% of the proposed facilities to support the mine are on federally owned U.S. Forest Service lands. The proposed project includes an underground mine, an ore processing mill (which will recover the gold without the use of cyanide), a tailings pond, and waste rock storage site, access roads, a work camp and transmission lines. The tailings pond, and waste rock storage site, access roads and a work camp would be on U.S. Forest Service lands (Gallatin and Shoshone National Forests).

The project would mine an estimated 1,800 tons of gold/silver/copper ore per day or an annual production rate of up to 500,000 tons of ore over a 10-15 year period. Reported proven reserves at the property are 2 million ounces of gold, 11 million ounces of silver, and 65,000 short tons of copper.[3] About 10% of the minable ore reserves are located on federal lands. According to Crown Butte representatives, the company has already invested over $32 million in the project, including reclaiming lands that were mined long before Crown Butte Mines began to explore for minerals in the area.[4]

## ENVIRONMENTAL CONCERNS

Environmental groups have detailed numerous concerns with the proposal. One of the major concerns is that the tailings impoundment facility in the mine plan could fail in the future due to earthquakes, avalanches or other events. Among the number of questions being raised by environmental groups are:

- What effect would the proposed project have on Yellowstone National Park?

[2] Noranda, Inc. is a diversified natural resource company with business activities in oil and gas, forest products, mining and metals. Noranda is listed on Canada's major stock exchanges.
[3] Platt's Metal Week, 29 July 1996, p.7.
[4] Crown Butte Mines, Inc. New World Project, Information Package, 1996

- How would the project affect wildlife, especially grizzly bears?
- Would tailings disposal at a different location have less environmental impact?

## Environmental Permitting

An extensive permitting process is directed to investigate these and other questions. The U.S. Forest Service (FS) has authority under the National Forest Act of 1976 to permit and regulate mining operations on its lands. A number of permits are required from the State of Montana that would, among other things, regulate air and water quality. Acquiring all the permits to operate the mine could prove to be time consuming and costly to the mining firm. Permits to operate the mine could be issued, issued with stipulations or denied. Without the required permits, the mine could not be developed. In compliance with state and federal regulations, site reclamation and reclamation bonding would be required for the project.

## The Environmental Impact Statement

In the case of the New World Project, the FS has required preparation of an environmental impact statement (EIS) under the National Environment Policy Act (NEPA) and Montana Environmental Policy Act guidelines. The EIS, begun in May 1993, will lead to one of three decisions: an approval of the application as submitted, an approval with modifications, or a no-action recommendation. A no-action recommendation would not necessarily prevent the project from going forward but would provide a baseline case from which to examine environmental impacts without the occurrence of mining. The draft EIS is expected toward the end of summer 1996. A panel of scientists has been established to provide expert review of the EIS once it is made available.

## U.N. World Heritage Action

The World Heritage Committee of the U.N. listed Yellowstone National Park a World Heritage site in 1978. The "in danger" listing came about because according to committee officials, "Yellowstone is considered threatened as a result of proposed gold, silver, and copper mining operations nearby, as well as by construction, logging and the growing number of visitors". An official committee vote was taken in December 1995 to place Yellowstone on its "in danger" list. Although the World Heritage Committee is in charge of approving sites nominated by the United States as World Heritage Sites--and can reach decisions on sites considered to be in danger-- it has no legal authority in any country. As park superintendent Marvin Jensen stated, the committee does not do anything but "list and delist."[5] Proponents for the project argue that this U.N. action was a public relations move to influence the outcome of the EIS currently underway. The president of Crown Butte Mines says that he could not accept the U.N. World Heritage Committee as a legitimate source for scientific review or determination of the viability of the project.[6]

# EXECUTIVE BRANCH AND CONGRESSIONAL OPTIONS

## Moratorium on Patents

In August 1995, President Clinton called for a moratorium on further mining patents on about 19,000 federally owned acres in the area. This was followed by a Notice of Proposed Withdrawal issued by the Department of the Interior (DOI) in late August 1995.[7] A moratorium on new patents would prevent the further transfer of mining claims to the private-sector, but patent applications in the pipeline that have received their first-half final approval would likely be honored. The moratorium segregates the land for up to two years while withdrawal of the lands is studied by the Bureau of Land Management (BLM). While the proposal is under study, patenting of claims is suspended, though the lands remain open to mineral leasing. Valid existing rights (claims that were located under the General Mining Law of 1872 prior to the withdrawal action) must be respected.

Withdrawal of these lands would not affect the site of the proposed New World project, but would curtail any expansion of the mine to adjoining federal lands not already claimed under the Mining Law. The Bureau of Land Management and the Forest Service held several field hearings in July

---

[5] Valarie Richardson, U.N. "Intrusion" Stirs Anger at Yellowstone, *The Washington Times,* February 1,1996, p. A 1.

[6] Crown Butte Yellowstone Project In Doubt, *Platts Metals Week,* December 11, 1995, p.

[7] See: Notice of Proposed Withdrawal: Montana, appearing in: Federal Register, Vol.60, No.170, Friday, September 1, 1995: p.45732.

1996 on the proposed withdrawal. The National Mining Association, meanwhile, has called the moratorium unnecessary and unwise.[8]

Withdrawals under the Federal Land Policy Management Act (FLPMA) have been used in the past to prevent mining activity on certain public lands. The Bureau of Land Management's stated mineral resource policy in part reads except for congressional withdrawals, public land shall remain open and available for mineral exploration and development unless withdrawal or other administrative action is clearly justified in the national interest." This policy has been criticized as making it difficult for land managers to close lands to mineral development, even in cases where there is a strong argument for doing so. Critics of the General Mining Law of 1872 believe that in many cases there is no way to protect other land values and uses short of withdrawal of lands from the operation of the Mining Law.

## Legislative Proposals

Legislation introduced by Sen. Bumpers (S. 1737) would prohibit new mining claims, patents and mineral leases on the federal land segregated by the Interior Department's NPW moratorium, subject to valid existing rights. Further, the bill would prohibit the Secretary of Agriculture from approving a plan of operation for mining that would pollute water flowing into Yellowstone National Park, the Clarks Fork of the Yellowstone National Wild and Scenic River or the Absaroka-Beartooth National Wilderness Area. The total area affected by S. 1737 is about 24,000 acres, none of it located in the present New World mine site.

In the House, proposed legislation (H.R. 1846) would establish the Yellowstone Headwaters Recreation Area and withdraw from mining certain lands upstream from the Park and also require the clean up of pollution from past mining. The Federal lands included in the proposal are currently open to location under the Mining Law.

Proponents of the mine believe that both House and Senate proposals would not affect the mine plan. Furthermore, they say, passage of the legislation would interfere with the environmental review process.

The House Resources Subcommittee on National Parks, Forests and Lands is expected to hold hearings this year on H.R. 1846 after the

---

[8] National Mining Association, *Mining Week*, September 5, 1995, p.1.

anticipated EIS is released. The analysis in the EIS will likely be considered at the hearings and may influence the prospects of the proposed legislation.

*Chapter 6*

# NEW WORLD GOLD MINE NEAR YELLOWSTONE: A PROJECT ABANDONED*

## *Marc Humphries*

## INTRODUCTION

Crown Butte Resources, Ltd. wanted to develop its New World gold mine deposit located near Yellowstone National Park. The proposed mine was located almost entirely on private property about 3 miles east of the northeast corner of Yellowstone National Park and next to the Absaroka-Beartooth Wilderness area. Pressure was applied at the state, federal and even international level to stop the project. On August 12, 1996, Crown Butte decided to cancel the project and enter into a "property exchange" agreement with the federal government. This chapter provides some background and details of the agreement by which Crown Butte will abandon the project and turn the property over to the federal government, in return for land which the company can sell to recover the investment made so far in the project.

---

* Excerpted from CRS Report 96-693 ENR.

## BACKGROUND

Crown Butte's New World mine would have produced an estimated 1,800 tons of gold/silver/copper ore per day (500,000 tons annually), valued at nearly $800 million over a 10-15 year period. An ore processing mill, a tailings pond, a waste rock storage site, access roads, a work camp and transmission lines were also planned.

The project stirred controversy because of its possible impacts on Yellowstone National Park and the surrounding area. Environmental groups opposed the project because of the potential for damage to water, recreational assets and wildlife. Crown Butte maintained it would employ "state-of-the-art" technology to contain waste in a proposed 106-acre tailings pond. Opponents of the project feared that the tailings pond might fail in the future due to earthquakes, avalanches or other events, and lead to acid mine drainage.

Most of the site was on leased private land that had previously been mined, which limited regulation of the project at the federal level. However, several permits from federal and especially state authorities would have been required to operate the mine and mill. Other potential barriers, not necessarily prohibitive, included an executive branch proposal to suspend patenting on federal lands surrounding the project, and proposed legislation (H.R. 1846, S. 1737) to halt it permanently. Public opponents to the mine included President Clinton. The United Nations World Heritage Committee, although it had no jurisdiction over the project, declared that it was a threat to Yellowstone Park.

## PROJECT ABANDONED

Because of permit delays, possible executive or legislative action, and public opposition, the economics of the project began to look less favorable. The broad opposition to the project apparently convinced the company that it could not -- or should not -- be completed.

On August 12, 1996, nearly six years after Crown Butte submitted its operating plan for the mine, its owners suspended permitting activities for the project. The suspension of permitting activity and the property exchange agreement were reached prior to final decisions made at the state and federal levels. A draft Environmental Impact Statement being prepared by the U.S. Forest Service, on whose land the tailings pond was planned, was expected by late summer, but now will not be issued.

## PROPERTY EXCHANGE AGREEMENT

Under the agreement, the U.S. government would trade other federal lands, yet to be identified but valued at $65 million, for Crown Butte's New World property interests. The company would then sell the land it received to recover the investment made so far in the project. An escrow account of $22.5 million would also be established by Crown Butte to fund ongoing restoration from earlier mining activity. As part of the agreement, Crown Butte would purchase the lands it is leasing, and include those lands in the package transferred to the government. The Forest Service would manage the lands received from Crown Butte.

*Chapter 7*

# Mining in National Parks and Wilderness Areas: Policy, Rules, Activity*

## *Duane A. Thompson*

## Introduction

The National Park Service and other agencies are responsible for protecting and preserving national parks and wilderness areas, while recognizing and accommodating mineral exploration and development. Although there has been some omnibus legislation enacted that provides uniform standards for use, many units are also protected by site specific provisions in their enacting legislation. These provisions are typically designed to meet the needs of a particular unit and protect its unique, often fragile, and irreplaceable features. This chapter provides a brief explanation how these conflicting and often intractable land use policies evolved. It provides a background on the general laws establishing national parks and wildernesses. Finally, it offers more detailed information on restrictions for mineral exploration and development applied to specific park and wilderness units.

---

* Excerpted from CRS Report 96-161 ENR.

Although the National Park Service and other agencies managing wilderness areas cannot deny access to mining claims by those having valid existing rights, they have authority to regulate development to control the impact on park, recreational, or wilderness values. Data show that 33 of 368 National Park System units have at least one mineral development activity occurring on them; at least 817 operations are ongoing, including 15 hardrock metals (primarily gold), 28 for sand, gravel, soil and similar substances, and 709 for nonfederal oil and gas. Conversely, available data suggests that there are no on-going mining operations in currently designated wilderness areas.

Since the establishment of the National Park and National Wilderness Preservation Systems, agencies of the Federal Government have faced the formidable task of reconciling two allowed, but fundamentally incompatible activities--hardrock mining and preserving lands as essentially untouched by development. Mining, usually involves major disturbance and sometimes permanent change of the environment, while management of national parks and wilderness areas seeks to minimize disruption of landscapes and wildlife habitats.

The competing demands for mineral extraction and land preservation/recreation have led to some of the more difficult and complex resource decisions faced by Federal policymakers. Today, vast highly-mineralized areas of the western United States, once coveted largely for their precious metals, are also highly regarded for their unique aesthetic values, habitats for endangered and other species, recreational use, or opportunity for solitude. Ironically, some of these areas are historic mining districts, that provided the raw materials for the industrial revolution in the mid-1800's. In many instances, servicing these mines stimulated the construction of railroads that later served the growing agricultural and commercial sectors of the Midwest and the Great Plains. More recently, however, the demand for raw materials and minerals to supply industrial needs has had to compete with or been supplanted by the demand for more recreational space, and the protection of woodlands and wildlife.

## BACKGROUND ON MINING AND PUBLIC LANDS

Historically, a major incentive for the private sector to invest in mineral development originated with the Mining Law of 1866, which declared all mineral lands of the public domain open to exploration and occupation.[1] The 1866 Mining Law was superseded by the now greatly debated General Mining Law of 1872. The concepts of conveying rights and land title, contained in the earlier Act, were generally included, but expanded by the 1872 Mining Law.[2] The Law states that:

> ...except as otherwise provided, all valuable mineral deposits in lands belonging to the United States, both surveyed and unsurveyed, shall be free and open to exploration and purchase, by citizens of the United States and those who have declared their intention to become such.

Individuals were assured exclusive rights to develop a mineral deposit upon location and establishment of value, and to profit solely from any development. In addition to mineral ownership passing to the claimant, the Mining Law contained provisions for title to the land (surface as well as subsurface) to pass to private hands as a "land patent." A claimant who has expended $500 worth of labor or improvement on a claim may apply for a patent and take title upon payment of either $5 or $2.50/acre depending on the type of claim--lode or placer, respectively. Other than requiring $100 annual expenditures (including value of work accomplished) by the claimant (to establish intent to develop) and assessing filing fees, the Federal Government did not participate in any profits from mineral development under the Mining Law. No royalties are paid to the Federal Government.[3]

The 1872 Mining Law did, however, differ from the earlier law by including the clause "except as otherwise provided," which expressly left the door open for subsequent limitations on mineral exploration and development. This language may have been a recognition by Congress that certain geological and geographical sites were so unique, fragile, and irreplaceable that they might be protected from any type of degradation, including mineral exploration and development. Only a few months earlier in 1872 Congress enacted legislation creating the first and one of our most magnificent national parks--Yellowstone.

The 1872 mineral disposal framework applied to virtually all minerals on Federal lands until 1920, when oil, natural gas, coal, and certain other

---

[1] Act of July 26, 1866, 14 Stat. 251. Maley, Terry S., Mining Law: From Location to Patent, Mineral Land Publications, P.O. Box 1186, Boise, Idaho, 1985, p. 6.
[2] Act of May 10, 1872; 17 Stat. 91; 30 USC 22. Inquiries involving legal issues relating to laws or regulations on mining in national parks or wildernesses may be referred to Ms. Pamela Baldwin, Legislative Attorney, American Law Division, Congressional Research Service.
[3] Some argue that the Federal government benefits from collection of corporate and income taxes associated with any mineral development. Others contest this concept.

bedded, defense related minerals were removed from location and patent laws and placed under a leasing system that required royalty payments to the Government.

The provisions of the early mining laws have led to litigation on many issues over the years. There is a substantial body of case law intended to interpret what originally may have been considered "simple" provisions and their application. Courts have been required to rule on such concepts as: the value and marketability of a mineral deposit; extra-lateral rights of a claimant or patentee; and whether a hypothetically "prudent man" would develop the ore body. For its part, when creating conservation areas, Congress has usually protected "valid existing rights." Determining what these are and reconciling mining with the laws establishing and protecting national parks and wilderness areas has been challenging, particularly with an almost infinite combination of geographic and legal circumstances associated with discovering, claiming, and patenting specific mineral deposits. Although legislative proposals have been introduced to clarify some of these issues, Congress, for the most part, has allowed the provisions of the laws to be interpreted through regulations and court decisions.

# NATIONAL PARKS

From the very beginning, the national parks were established for current recreation and educational use while protecting them for the future. According to the Department of the Interior:

Congress charged the national Park Service (NPS) with the responsibility of managing the various units that comprise the national Park System so as to preserve and protect the resources and values of those units for current and future generations.[4]

To achieve this goal of protection, the NPS has a number of management tools at its disposal. These include prohibiting certain activities, regulating activities to reduce their adverse effects, and purchasing private lands and/or mineral rights to prevent the onset of such activities. Consistent with the Park Service's mandate, when most park units[5] are created, the lands are withdrawn from mineral entry at that time.

---

[4] U. S. Dept. of the Interior, National Park Service. Mineral Laws and Regulations and the National Park System. Natural Resource Report NPS / MMB / NRR-89 / 01. Washington, D C: Dec. 1989. p. 1; see also 16 U.S.C. §1 and la-1.

[5] Park units include not only National Parks, but also National Monuments, National Recreation Areas, National Rivers, some Wild and Scenic Rivers, National Historic Parks, National

However, the value of a park or wilderness, particularly in the West with its dry air and distant vistas, may be affected by the lands beyond the area's boundaries. Federal efforts to preserve the unspoiled nature of an area may be affected by activities including mineral development on adjacent or nearby lands over which the NPS or other Federal agencies have little direct control, absent acquisition or condemnation of the lands--an often lengthy and expensive process.

An example of land acquisition to protect park values has occurred at a nearby unit. While standing on a rock outcrop at Harpers Ferry, Thomas Jefferson remarked that the view was worth crossing an ocean to see. Consequently, the Harpers Ferry National Historic Park has sought to acquire property rights, whether full title or scenic easement, to all lands within eyesight of "Jefferson Rock," some of which are several miles distant, to prevent commercial and residential development that arguably would destroy the scenic view.

Buffer zones have occasionally been proposed in which development activities that would detract from the aesthetic or natural values of an area could be either restricted or prevented altogether. This concept is very controversial and no legislation directly authorizing buffer zones has been enacted.

Typically, lands within the National Park System have been withdrawn from new mineral entry or location. However, many of the national parks and monuments were established with ongoing mining operations or other valid existing rights. Such rights may permit the holder to explore on or develop minerals in a claim or on patented lands, within park boundaries. A valid existing right may also exist in situations where privately-owned minerals underlie a federally-owned surface--the so-called "split estate." Holders of valid claims and patents may exercise their rights to develop the minerals, "subject to such regulations prescribed by the Secretary of the Interior as he deems necessary or desirable for the preservation and management of those areas."[6] According to the Bureau of Land Management (BLM), the location of a claim inside a park unit does not invalidate the right to go to patent. The BLM is only concerned whether the applicant has met the tests (marketability, etc.) to go to patent, first at the time the park is established and second, at the time application for patent is made.

In 1976, Congress enacted the "Mining in Parks Act" (P.L. No. 94-429, 16 U.S.C. 1901 et seq). This Act found and established as a matter of policy

---

Scenic Riverways, National Rivers and Recreation Areas, National Historic Parks and Preserves, National Seashores, and National Preserves.
[6] 16 U.S.C. §1902.

that, because of changes in mining technology, the continued application of the mining laws to areas of the National Park System conflicts with the purposes for which they were established and that all mining operations in areas of the National Park System should be conducted to prevent and minimize damage. The exercise of valid existing mineral rights on both patented or unpatented mining claims in System units was made subject to regulations the Secretary of the Interior deems "necessary or desirable for the preservation and management" of those areas. The ability to regulate mining varies, depending on the nature of the mining rights--generally there is less Federal control over lands fully owned by private parties than over unpatented mining claims.

The Act also required the recording of outstanding mining claims within System units and established a presumption of abandonment for claims that were not recorded. The payment of compensation was authorized for any owner found by a court to have suffered a taking of property compensable under the Constitution. However, according to the Geologic Resources Division of the National Park Service, recorded claims are presumed to be valid unless they are invalidated at either (1) the time the park unit is established, or (2) the time of the patent application. The Resources Division estimated total unpatented claims at 12,428 as of January 1995. In addition to this large number of unpatented claims, the Park System also contains 746 valid mineral patents.

Largely because of valid mineral rights existing when the NPS units were created, mining occurs in some national parks. The general mining regulations for national parks are contained in Title 36, Part 9, Subpart A (Mining and Mining Claims) and Subpart B (Nonfederal Oil and Gas Rights) of the Code of Federal Regulations (C.F.R.). Subpart A regulations cover a broad range of topics including, but not limited to: access permits (§9.3); surface disturbance moratorium (§9.4); recordation of mining claims (§9.5); transfer of interests (§9.6); assessment work (§9.7); use of water (§9.8); plan of [mining] operation (§9.9); plan approval (§9.10); reclamation requirements (§9.11); supplementation or revision of plan of operations (§9.12); performance bonds (§9.13); appeals (§9.14); use of roads by commercial vehicles (§9.15); penalties (§9.16); public inspection of documents (§9.17); and surface use and patent restrictions (§9.18). Subpart B. (Nonfederal Oil and Gas Rights) contains provisions similar to those above plus requirements unique to oil and gas well safety and proper disposal of well wastes.

The following table 1 lists national park units that have special mineral provisions, identifies relevant regulations for mining in the parks, and provides the most recent available information on the status of mining in the listed areas. It shows that 33 of 368 National Park System units have at least one mining activity occurring on them; at least 817 operations are ongoing, including 15 hardrock metals (primarily gold), 28 for sand, gravel, soil and similar substances, and 709 for nonfederal oil and gas.[7]

**Table 1.** National Park System Units with Special Mineral Provisions

| Name | Special Provisions | On-going Operations |
|---|---|---|
| Bering Land Bridge NP, Alaska | Part 9; Subparts A & B | 5 (gold) |
| Kenai Fjords NP, Alaska | ditto (do) | 1 (gold) |
| Cape Krusenstern NM, Alaska | do | 1 (sand and gravel) |
| Lake Clark NP, Alaska | do | 1 (gold) |
| Wrangell-St. Elias NP, Alaska | do | 2 (gold) |
| Gauley River NRA, W. Va. | do | 11 (nonfederal oil and gas) |
| New River Gorge NR, W. Va. | do | 1 (coal); 2 (nonfederal oil and gas) |
| Upper Delaware, New York | do | 5 (sand and gravel) |
| Cuyahoga Valley NRA, Ohio | do | 1 (clay) |
| Hopewell Culture NHP, Ohio | do | 1 (sand and gravel) |
| Saint Croix NSR, Wisc. | do | 5 (sand and gravel) |
| Acadia NP, Maine | do | 1 (sand and gravel) |
| Lake Chelan NRA, Washington | do | 3 (sand and gravel) |
| Ross Lake NRA, Washington | do | 3 (sand and gravel); 1 (topsoil) |
| Curecanti NRA, Colorado | do | 1 (decomposed granite) |
| Big Cypress NPr, Florida | do | 30 (nonfederal oil and gas) |
| Big South Fork NR&RA, Tennessee | do | 210 (nonfederal oil and gas) |
| Chattahoochee River NRA, Georgia | do | 2 (sand and gravel) |
| Obed Wild and Scenic River, Tennessee | do | 2 (undisclosed); 244 (nonfederal oil and gas) |
| Alibates Flint Quarries NM, Texas | do | 1 (nonfederal oil and gas) |

[7] Total number of national park units was retrieved from the National Park Service Website, "http://www.nps.gov/nps/"

| Name | Special Provisions | On-going Operations |
|------|-------------------|---------------------|
| Aztec Ruins NM, New Mexico | do | 3 (nonfederal oil and gas) |
| Big Thicket NP, Texas | do | 2 (sand); 15 (nonfederal oil and gas) |
| El Malpais NM, New Mexico | do | 1 (cinder) |
| Hot Springs NP, Arkansas | do | 1 (novaculite) |
| Jean Lafitte NGP & Pr, Louisiana | do | 1 (nonfederal oil and gas) |
| Lake Meredith NRA, Texas | do | 180 (nonfederal oil and gas) |
| Padre Island NS, Texas | CFR §7.75(h)-- Mineral exploration and extraction. Regulations for the scope of mineral extraction, exercise of nonfederal and gas rights, and applicability of state laws. 14 (nonfederal oil and gas) | |
| Poverty Point NM, Louisiana Part 9; Subparts A & B 12 (nonfederal oil and gas) | | |
| Salinas Pueble Mission NM, New Mexico | do | 1 (stone) |
| Death Valley NP, California/Nevada | CFR §7.26(a) through (e)--Limits claims mining purposes only, provides restrictions for road construction and water use. | 1 (borax); 1 (gold). 20 (unspecified) |
| Joshua Tree NP, California | Part 9; Subparts A & B | 1 (garnet and epkidote); 4 (precious metals) |
| Mojave NPr. California | do | 28 (unspecified) |
| Saguaro NP, Arizona | do | 1 (wulfenite and gold) |

# WILDERNESS AREAS

The Wilderness Act created the National Wilderness Preservation System in 1964, set out appropriate management direction, and was the first of many laws (total of 117 laws from 1964 through 1995) designating wilderness areas. The 1964 Act included a general policy statement for the use of designated wilderness areas:[8]

**Table 2.** Major Wilderness Laws

| Title | Public Law # | Date | Brief Description of Major Provisions |
|---|---|---|---|
| The Wilderness Act | P.L. 88-577 | 1964.00 | -special prov. allowed for mining on valid claims and mineral development on leases established before Dec.. 31, 1983 |
| "Eastern Wilderness Act" | P.L. 93-622 | 1975.00 | -designated roadless areas in the East should be included and managed as part of the NWPS |
| Federal Land Policy and Management Act | P.L. 94-579 | 1976.00 | -existing loses such as mining, mineral leasing...permitted to continue in study areas subject to regulations set by the Secretary of the Interior. |
| Endangered American Wilderness Act | P.L. 95-237 | 1978.00 | -criteria for assignment changed to encourage the establishment of wilderness areas near large cities even though some of these areas had previously been influenced by man |
| Alaska National Interest Lands Conservation Act (ANILCA) | P.L. 96-487 | 1980.00 | -use of certain vehicles authorized and wilderness cabins to be maintained with some new cabins added |
| Colorado Wilderness Act | P.L. 96-560 1980.00 | | -prohibited establishment of buffer zones around wildernesses --provided for release of remaining wilderness study areas to traditional management planning and uses |

In order to assure that an increasing population, accompanied by expanding settlement and growing mechanization, does not occupy and

---

[8] P.L. 88-577 (16 U.S.C. §§ 1131-1136), Section 2(a).

modify all areas within the United States and its possessions, leaving no lands designated for preservation and protection in their natural condition, it is hereby declared to be the policy of the Congress to secure for the American people of present and future generations the benefits of an enduring resource of wilderness.

Unlike national park lands, which are exclusively under the jurisdiction of he National Park Service in the Department of the Interior, wilderness areas, as stated in the Act, "shall continue to be managed by the Department and agency having jurisdiction thereover immediately before its inclusion in the National Wilderness Preservation System...." Consequently, lands in the wilderness system can be administered by Departments other than Interior (e.g., he Department of Agriculture, in the case of wilderness areas under the auspices of the Forest Service) and by other agencies within the Interior department (e.g., the U.S. Fish and Wildlife Service and the Bureau of Land Management). A brief list of some of the major legislation expanding the wilderness system is contained in the table below. Many other statutes have designated wilderness areas.

Generally, Congress permitted mineral-related activities in designated wilderness areas for 20 years following the enactment of the Wilderness Act in 1964. During that period, new mineral rights could be established. However, following December 31, 1983, new mineral rights could no longer be established, although Congress did permit prospecting in designated wilderness areas.[9] Valid existing mineral rights, some of which may have been established during the 20-year grace period, may still be exercised and developed in designated areas, subject to reasonable regulations to protect the wilderness character of the lands.[10]

Some literature asserts that mining in wilderness areas is an extremely complex legal issue, and that regulating exploration and mining activities is site-specific.[11] Maintaining the unspoiled character of wilderness can be especially confounded in the East, where the mineral estate has often been

[9] The authority to establish new mineral rights in existing wilderness areas was actually terminated on September 30, 1981, through riders on the Dept. of the Interior Appropriations Acts for FY1982, FY1983, and FY1984.

[10] Mineral development has occurred in some national forest wilderness areas, but a comprehensive list of such developments is not available. Personal communication with Tom Klabunde, Legislative Affairs Staff, U.S.D.A. Forest Service, Washington, D.C., on December 5, 1995.

[11] Browning, James A., John C. Hendee, and Joe W. Roggenbuck, 103 Wilderness Laws: Milestones and Management Direction in Wilderness Legislation 1964-1987, University of Idaho, College of Forestry, Wildlife and Range Sciences, Bulletin No. 51, October, 1988, pp. 6 and 7.

split from the surface estate.[12] Although the surface of a wilderness may be under the authority of a particular agency, the subsurface rights may have been severed and reside in private ownership. In these instances, a question of access for mineral development often arises. The Federal agencies generally cannot deny access to privately held mineral estate, but can regulate mineral activities to varying degrees.

Congress has generally pursued a situational approach and has adopted several approaches to mineral development. Congress has sought either to accommodate mineral development by drawing the boundaries of the wilderness to exclude highly-mineralized, potentially-developable areas or to avoid development by acquiring mining rights through purchase or exchange. The following Table 3. identifies wilderness areas and/or laws that contain special provisions on mining. As noted, no ongoing mining operations are currently occurring in wilderness areas.

**Table 3.** Wilderness Areas with Special Mining Provisions

| Name | Special Provisions | On-going Operations |
|------|--------------------|--------------------|
| River of No Return Wilderness. | The Central Idaho Wilderness Act of 1980, P.L. 96-312. Prospecting, exploration and development of mining of cobalt and associated minerals in the Clear Creek Special Mining Management Zone of the River of No Return Wilderness shall be permitted beyond the December 31, 1983 deadline, subject to regulations. | None noted. |
| San Rafael Wilderness P.L. 90-271 | Wilderness Act of 1964. | None noted. |
| San Gabriel Wilderness P.L. 90-318. | Wilderness Act of 1964. | None noted. |
| Sawtooth National Recreation Area, P.L. 92-400. | The Secretary may acquire mineral interests in lands within the recreation area (which includes the wilderness) with or without the consent of the owner. Subject to valid existing rights, all federal entry, and patent under the U.S. mining law. | None noted. |

---

[12] U.S. General Accounting Office. Private Mineral Rights Complicate the Management of Eastern Wilderness Areas. GAO/RCED-84-101. Washington, D.C.: U.S. Govt. Print. Off., July 26, 1984. 48 pp.

| Name | Special Provisions | On-going Operations |
|------|--------------------|---------------------|
| Hells Canyon National Recreation Area, P.L. 94-199. | do. | None noted. |
| The Endangered American Wilderness Act of 1978, P.L. 95-237. | Extends the mineral exploration, patenting, and development period for the Gospel-Hump Wilderness from December 31, 1983, to December 31, 1988. | None noted. |
| Boundary Waters Canoe Area Wilderness, P.L. 95-495. | No mining of minerals owned by the U.S. is permitted; no exploration or mining of nonfederal minerals is permitted if such action would adversely affect navigable waters. The Secretary may acquire minerals and mineral rights owned by the private sector. Specific guidelines are provided for any mining activity or acquisition of minerals rights. | None noted. |
| The Alaska National Interest Lands Conservation Act, P.L. 96-487. | (Misty Fjords National Monument Wilderness) The Secretary of Agriculture shall allow installation, maintenance, and use of navigation aids, docking facilities, and staging and transfer facilities associated with the development of the mineral deposit at Quartz Hill. Such activities shall not include mineral extraction, milling. or processing | None noted. |
| Monongahela National Forest, P.L. 97-466. | (a) Exploration activities, including core drilling and use of mechanized ground equipment, is allowed in the Cranberry Wilderness to determine the value of the nonfederally owned mineral resources there, under regulations set by the Secretary of agriculture. (b) The Secretary of the Interior is directed to acquire nonfederal owned coal deposits and other minerals interests and rights within the Cranberry Wilderness, and such interests and rights outside the wilderness according to certain requirements Guidelines are provided for the acquisition of these mineral interests and rights. | None noted. |

| Name | Special Provisions | On-going Operations |
|------|--------------------|---------------------|
| The Vermont Wilderness Act, P.L. 98-322. | All federally-owned lands within the White Rocks National Recreation Area Which includes portions of the big Branch and Peru Peak Wildernesses) are withdrawn from all forms of appropriation under the mineral and geothermal leasing laws. | None noted. |
| California Wilderness Act of 1984, P.L. 98-425. | Various sites within California. Mineral prospecting, exploration, development, and mining are permitted in the North Fork Smith Roadless Area under laws applicable to nonwilderness national forest lands. | None noted. |
| The Florida Wilderness Act of 1984, P.L. 98-430. | Specifies that phosphate leases shall not be permitted on Osceola National Forest (which includes the Big Gum Swamp Wilderness) unless: the President defines need; there is a procedure for public input; the President specifies impacts; the President specifies conditions and stipulations to govern any mining activity; Congress approves the President's recommendation by joint resolution. | None noted. |
| The Wyoming Wilderness Act of 1984, P.L. 98-550. | Oil and gas exploration and development activities on the Palisades Wilderness Study Areas shall be administered under reasonable conditions to protect the environment under regulations and laws generally applicable to non-wilderness lands. Subject to valid misting rights, the Palisades Wilderness Study Area is withdrawn from all forms of appropriation under the mining laws. | None noted. |
| The Pennsylvania Wilderness Act of 1984, P.L. 98-585. | The Secretary of Agriculture is authorized to acquire land, including oil, gas, and mineral interests or scenic easements, within the wildernesses by various means. | None noted. |

| Name | Special Provisions | On-going Operations |
|---|---|---|
| Arizona Desert Wilderness Act of 1990, P.L. 101-628 | Private mineral rights within wilderness areas designated by this tie be acquired as expeditiously as possible by the Secretary using existing authority to acquire such rights by exchange. | None noted. |
| Los Padres Condor Range and River Protection Act, P.L. 102-301 | (a) Subject to valid existing rights, federal owned lands depicted a map entitled "Mineral Withdrawal Area, California Coastal Zone, Big Sur-- Proposed are general withdrawn from mineral entry. (b) Subject to valid existing rights, all mining claims located within the withdrawal area shall be subject to such regulations as the Secretary of Agriculture may prescribe to ensure that mining will be consistent with the protection of scenic, scientific, cultural, and other resources of the area. In instances where a land patent is issued following the date of enactment only title to the minerals will be conveyed. | None noted. |
| El Malpais National Monument, P.L. 100-225. | Section 504 provides for the Secretary of the Interior to exchange Federal mineral interests for private mineral interests--both described in detail within the section. | None noted. |
| Washington Park Wilderness Act of 1988, P.L. 100-688. | Subject to valid existing rights, the lands within recreation areas are withdrawn from...disposal...under the United States mining laws, and disposition under the United States mineral leasing laws: Provided, however, That within that portion of the Lake Chelan National Recreation Area which is not designated as wilderness, salad, rock and gravel may be made available for sale to the residents of Stehekin for local use.... | None noted. |

*Chapter 8*

# WORLD HERITAGE CONVENTION AND U.S. NATIONAL PARKS[*]

## *Lois McHugh*

## INTRODUCTION

On March 6, 2001, Congressman Don Young introduced H.R. 883, the American Land Sovereignty Act. H.R. 883 requires congressional approval to add any lands owned by the United States to the World Heritage List, a UNESCO-administered list established by the 1972 World Heritage Convention. Two years ago, on May 20, 1999, the House passed (by voice vote) an identical bill also numbered H.R. 883, but the legislation did not pass in the Senate. Sponsors of that bill expressed concern that adding a U.S. site to the U.N. list, which is currently done under executive authority, might not protect the rights of private property owners or the states. The Clinton Administration and opponents of the bill argued that the designation has no effect on property rights and does not provide the United Nations with any legal authority over U.S. territory. In related legislation, P.L. 106-429, in which H.R. 5526, the Foreign Operations, Export Financing, and Related Programs appropriations act for 2001 was referenced, contained language prohibiting funding from this bill for the United Nations World Heritage Fund. The FY2000 contribution to the Fund was $450,000. The World

---

[*] Excerpted from CRS Report 96-395 F.

Heritage Fund provides technical assistance to countries requesting help in protecting World Heritage sites. This paper describes the operation of the UNESCO Convention and will be updated periodically. This legislation would also affect U.S. participation in the UNESCO Man and the Biosphere Program, which includes some of the same sites.

There are currently 690 natural and cultural sites in 122 countries listed on the World Heritage List established under the World Heritage Convention. Twenty U.S. sites are listed, including Yellowstone and Grand Canyon National Parks, Independence Hall, and the Statue of Liberty. The World Heritage in Danger list currently has 30 sites in 24 countries, including Yellowstone National Park and Everglades National Park. Yellowstone National Park was listed on the sites in danger list in 1995 and the Everglades was listed in 1993. The 1980 National Historic Preservation Act establishes the Interior Department as the administrator and coordinator of U.S. activities under the Convention. H.R. 883, the American Land Sovereignty Act, would place conditions on Interior's authority to nominate new sites and require specific congressional authorization for new nominations.

## ABOUT THE CONVENTION

The Convention Concerning the Protection of the World Cultural and Natural Heritage, popularly known as the World Heritage Convention, was adopted by the General Conference of the United Nations Educational, Scientific, and Cultural Organization (UNESCO) in 1972. The United States initiated and led the development of the treaty and was the first nation to ratify it in 1973. Currently, 162 nations are parties to the Convention. The Convention's purpose is to identify and list worldwide natural and cultural sites and monuments considered to be of such exceptional interest and such universal value that their protection is the responsibility of all mankind. Each country adopting the Convention pledges to protect listed sites and monuments within its borders and refrain from activities which harm World Heritage sites in other countries. The Convention states in Article 4 that each party to it "recognizes that the duty of ensuring the identification, protection, conservation, presentation and transmission to future generations of the cultural and natural heritage .... situated on its territory, belongs primarily to that state."[1] The international community agrees to help protect them through the World Heritage Committee and Fund.

## WORLD HERITAGE COMMITTEE AND FUND

The World Heritage Committee, composed of 21 specialists from member nations elected for 6-year terms, administers the Convention. (The United States was mostly recently a member of the Committee for a term ending October 1999). The Committee has two principal tasks. First, it recognizes the sites nominated by member states to be included on the World Heritage List, based on the criteria established by the Committee. Decisions on additions to the List are generally made by consensus. UNESCO provides administrative assistance to the Committee but has no role in its decisions. The Committee monitors the sites and when a site is seriously endangered, it may be put on a List of World Heritage in Danger after consultation with the country in which the site is located. In 1992, the Committee adopted a plan to improve its operations, including an increased focus on monitoring conditions at existing sites rather than adding new sites to the List.

The Committee also administers the World Heritage Fund, which provides technical and financial aid to countries requesting assistance. Assistance can include such support as expert studies, training, and equipment for protection. World Heritage Fund technical assistance must be requested by a member country in an agreement with the Committee, which sets conditions for the assistance. The World Heritage Fund receives income from several sources. Member states pay dues equal to 1% of their UNESCO contribution. The United States is not a member of UNESCO and therefore does not contribute as a member. The Fund also receives voluntary contributions from governments, donations from institutions, individuals, and from national or international promotional activities. The United States contributed $450,000 voluntarily to this program in FY2000, an amount appropriated in the Foreign Operations Appropriation. A similar contribution was requested for FY2001. This contribution was prohibited by P.L. 106-429. Virtually no other U.S. money was contributed to this program.

---

[1] Convention concerning the protection of the world cultural and natural heritage. 27 UST 37.

# U.S. PARTICIPATION

The National Park Service is the primary U.S. contact for World Heritage sites in the United States. The National Historic Preservation Act Amendment of 1980 (P.L. 96-515) charges the Department of Interior with coordinating and directing U.S. activities under the Convention, in cooperation with the Departments of State, Commerce, and Agriculture, the Smithsonian Institution, and the Advisory Council on Historic Preservation. The National Park Service administers all the U.S. sites with funds appropriated by Congress, except for several that are owned by states, a foundation, and an Indian tribe.

# LEGISLATION

## American Land Sovereignty Protection Act

H.R. 883 was introduced by Representative Don Young on March 6, 2001, and referred to the Committee on Resources. It has 30 cosponsors. The legislation amends the National Historic Preservation Act of 1980 (P.L. 96-515) to require a determination by the Interior Department that the designation of a new site will not adversely affect private land within ten miles of the site, a report to Congress on the impact of the designation on existing and future uses of the land and surrounding private land, and specific authorization by Congress for new World Heritage site designations. The bill also terminates and prohibits unauthorized designation of biosphere reserves under the UNESCO Man and the Biosphere Program.

## Foreign Operations, Export Financing, and Related Appropriations Act, 2001

(P.L. 106-429, as passed by Congress, enacted by reference in H.R. 5526.) Section 580 of this bill states that none of the funds appropriated or made available by this Act may be provided for the U.S. contribution to the United Nations World Heritage Fund. P.L. 106-429 was signed by the President on November 6, 2000.

# ISSUES FOR CONGRESS

## Impact of the Convention on U.S. Sovereignty

Although the debate on the American Land Sovereignty Protection bill was often couched in terms which included U.N. influence over U.S. parks and monuments, supporters of the American Land Sovereignty Protection Act were primarily concerned that a lack of a congressional role in designating the sites and a lack of congressional oversight of implementation of the act undermines the congressional role under the Constitution to make rules governing land belonging to the United States. As the House Resources Committee web site on the legislation stated: "By using these international designations, the Executive Branch is able to guide domestic land use policies without consulting Congress."[2] Supporters express concern that even though there may be no international or U.N. direct control of U.S. sites, federal agency managers may take into account the international rules of the World Heritage program in making land use decisions, or use the designation to undermine local land use decisions, often without the advice or even the knowledge of local authorities or property owners.

The World Heritage Convention does not give the United Nations authority over U.S. sites. The Department of State has testified that under the terms of the World Heritage Convention, management and sovereignty over the sites remain with the country where the site is located. Supporters of the World Heritage system note that member countries nominate sites for the World Heritage List voluntarily and agree to develop laws and procedures to protect them using their own constitutional procedures. Most of the U.S. sites named have already been accorded protection in law as national monuments or parks. In commenting on the bill, the Clinton Administration stated that the designation does not give the United Nations the authority to affect land management decisions within the United States and has not been utilized to exclude Congress from land management decisions. The Department of State noted that the Convention itself has no role or authority beyond listing sites and offering technical advice and assistance. Supporters of the convention assert that World Heritage status has been the impetus behind closer cooperation between federal agencies and state and local authorities.

---

[2] U.S. Congress. House. Committee on Resources. [http://www. house.gov/ resources/ 106[th]cong/fullcomm/sovereignty.htm].

# IMPACT OF PLACEMENT ON THE
# WORLD HERITAGE LIST

Inclusion on the World Heritage List increases knowledge and interest in sites throughout the world. Many countries use the World Heritage designation to increase tourism to site areas. Designation also brings international attention and support to protect endangered sites. In 1993, the World Heritage Committee supported the United States in protecting Glacier Bay National Park and Preserve by publicizing U.S. concerns about a Canadian open pit mine near the Bay and reminding the Canadian government of its obligations under the Convention to protect the site. In 1996, international concern, including concern raised by U.S. citizens, was instrumental in changing the plans of a Polish company to build a shopping center near Auschwitz Concentration Camp in Poland, a World Heritage Site. In March of 2000, Mexico dropped plans to develop a salt plant on the shores of a gray whale breeding ground in a protected Mexican area designated as a World Heritage Site.

Supporters of legislation restricting U.S. World Heritage participation express concern about the impact of the designation on private property near the sites. They suggest that agreeing to manage the site in accordance with the international convention may have an impact on the use of private land nearby, or may even be an indirect way of complying with treaties which the Congress has not approved. They claim that advocacy groups use federal regulations and international land use designations to frustrate the public land management decision-making process. The Interior Department has testified, on the other hand, that the nomination procedure includes open public meetings and congressional notification on sites being considered.

# YELLOWSTONE NATIONAL PARK

In June 1995, the U.S. Department of the Interior notified the World Heritage Committee that Yellowstone was in danger and requested an on-site visit. In a follow up letter, the Department of the Interior noted actions which the United States was taking to address the situation. A team organized by the World Heritage Center reviewed actual and potential threats to the park. In December 1995, based on this visit and consultations with U.S. government officials, the World Heritage Committee placed Yellowstone on the List of World Heritage in Danger, citing threats posed by plans for a gold mine just over 1 mile from the Park, the introduction of non-native fish into Yellowstone Lake, and activities to eliminate brucellosis from Park bison herds. The World Heritage Committee noted that any response to the threat was a U.S. domestic decision and asked that the U.S. government keep the committee informed of actions taken by the United States and to assess what more must be done in order to remove Yellowstone from the endangered list.

Both the non native fish and the Park bison herds are the subject of ongoing federal, state, and local discussions. The gold mine issue has been resolved. Congress appropriated funds to compensate the mine owners for not developing it. The non-native fish problem is ultimately unresolvable, but Park authorities are working to minimize the number of non native fish in Yellowstone lake. The Administration will continue to report annually to the World Heritage Committee on both Yellowstone and Everglades National Parks until they are removed from the endangered list. The World Heritage Committee will continue to list both parks on the World Heritage in Danger List in consultation with the United States. The December meeting of the World Heritage Committee will be the next opportunity for the United States to report on actions taken to eliminate the danger to the parks, or to discuss changes to their designation. It is too early to know what the Bush Administration position will be on this topic.

*Chapter 9*

# NATIONAL PARK SERVICE: ACTIONS NEEDED TO IMPROVE TRAVEL COST MANAGEMENT[*]

## *McCoy Williams*

## INTRODUCTION

The Park Service reported that it incurred from $39 million to $50 million, in inflation-adjusted dollars annually, on travel costs during the past 4 fiscal years, but it does not know its actual costs for foreign travel or the travel costs related to attending conferences because its does not routinely record this required information.

The *Federal Travel Regulation* requires that agency travel accounting systems capture certain data, including travel type, such as foreign or domestic travel, and purpose, such as training or conference attendance. In addition, the Park Service requires that all vouchers for foreign travel be processed at its Accounting Operations Center, but this policy is not consistently followed. The current procedures for processing travel vouchers and recording travel costs make it difficult for the Park Service to report reliable travel data that are consistent with the *Federal Travel Regulation*. Officials at the Park Service told us that they are implementing a new travel

[*] Excerpted from General Accounting Office Report GAO-03-354. February 2003.

management system that will track travel type and purpose. The system is expected to be operating throughout the agency by approximately September 2003.

Reliable, detailed travel information that is consistent with the *Federal Travel Regulation* is critical so that the Park Service and the Congress can perform their respective roles and responsibilities with regard to efficient travel cost management.

**Park Service Reported Total Travel Costs, Fiscal Years 1999-2002, Actual and Adjusted for Inflation to 2001 Dollars**

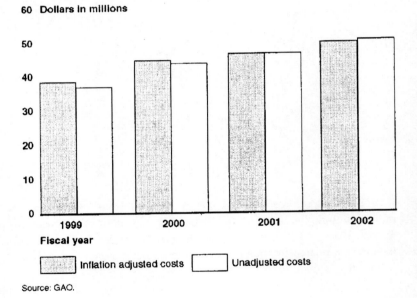

Source: GAO.

**Note:** This figure represents GAO's analysis of data provided by the National Park Service.

Unable to obtain information on the National Park Service's (Park Service) travel costs, the Subcommittee asked in its June 3, 2002, letter and subsequent discussions that we review several issues pertaining to the Park Service's travel costs. As principal steward over 385 areas covering 84 million acres of land, the Park Service receives approximately 25 percent of the Department of the Interior's (DOI) annual appropriations. In fiscal year 2001, the net cost of Park Service operations was over $2 billion, and included travel and transportation costs of almost $47 million.

To assess the availability of the Park Service's travel expense information, the Subcommittee asked us to determine (1) whether the Park Service could provide its travel cost by type (such as foreign or domestic) and purpose (such as conference attendance or training) for fiscal years 1999, 2000, 2001, and 2002, and if not, what factors contribute to the Park Service's inability to provide the information, (2) the annual total travel costs for those years, and (3) how many foreign trips were authorized for those 4 fiscal years and at what estimated cost. Further, we were to describe the Park Service's authorization process for foreign travel.

## RESULTS IN BRIEF

The Park Service does not know its actual costs for foreign travel or the travel costs related to attending conferences because it does not routinely record this required information. Information generated from the Park Service's travel accounting system is not consistent with the *Federal Travel Regulation*,[1] which requires agencies to track the type (such as foreign or domestic) and purpose (such as conference attendance) of official government travel.[2] In addition, while the Park Service requires all vouchers for foreign travel to be processed at its Accounting Operations Center (AOC), this policy is not consistently followed. Although enforcement of this policy would not automatically yield summary information on foreign travel costs under the existing travel accounting system, it could facilitate the enhancements necessary for tracking and monitoring Park Service foreign travel costs. The current procedures for processing travel vouchers and recording travel expenditures include a combination of both centralized and decentralized methods. One result of this is that the Park Service records certain foreign travel costs as domestic travel costs. Therefore, it is difficult for the Park Service to report reliable travel data that are consistent with the *Federal Travel Regulation*.

Reliable detailed travel information that is consistent with the *Federal Travel Regulation* is critical so that the Park Service, the Congress, and the General Services Administration (GSA)[3] can perform their respective roles

---

[1] Title 41 C.F.R. 300-304. The *Federal Travel Regulation* is issued by the General Services Administration, in part, to provide guidance to agencies on the authorization of travel reimbursement for certain federal government civilian employees when traveling on official government business.

[2] 41 C.F.R. 301-71.2 and appendix C to Chapter 301 identify required data elements.

[3] GSA's Office of Governmentwide Policy is responsible for the *Federal Travel Regulation*, which provides travel policy for federal government agencies and their travelers.

and responsibilities with regards to efficient travel cost management. The Park Service is in the process of implementing a new travel management system that is designed to generate travel information in accordance with the *Federal Travel Regulation* and will eventually be able to provide reliable detailed travel information on foreign travel costs and costs for attending conferences. This system is expected to be operational throughout the Park Service by approximately September 2003.

After adjusting for inflation, total reported Park Service travel costs for the past 3 years have increased by an average of about 9 percent annually from approximately $39 million in fiscal year 1999, to approximately $50 million in fiscal year 2002. The Park Service was able to provide overall travel costs broken down by its seven regions, the Washington, D.C., office, and its other reporting units for fiscal years 1999 through 2002. Travel costs for the Washington, D.C., office rose by approximately 60 percent, increasing from $5.6 million to over $9 million. Combined travel costs for the seven regional offices increased approximately 26 percent, from almost $31 million to almost $39 million. The three remaining units, which include the service centers and the Job Corps Program, decreased slightly, going from almost $2.5 million to almost $2.4 million.

Given the Park Service's failure to record and thus inability to confidently report foreign trips and the related costs, the Park Service's Office of International Affairs (OIA) provided us estimated trip and cost data. Based on the authorization documents that it receives approximately 6 weeks prior to travel dates, OIA estimated a steadily increasing number of trips from 355 in 1999 to 470 in 2002. It acknowledged that some foreign trips may not have actually occurred, and that cost data could be suspect for this reason as well as because trips may have been extended or shortened since approval. The Park Service's foreign travel approval process largely entails various levels of supervisor and agency approval and ends with the Department of State and appropriate U.S. embassy concurrences.

This chapter makes recommendations for the Park Service to (1) establish procedures for capturing travel data, including travel type and purpose as required by the *Federal Travel Regulation*, (2) enforce the existing Park Service foreign travel policy that requires all foreign travel vouchers to be processed electronically by AOC, and (3) address Joint Financial Management Improvement Program (JFMIP)[4] *Travel System*

*Requirements* when designing and implementing the travel system scheduled for completion later this year as well as any future travel systems.

In written comments on a draft of this report, DOI concurred with our conclusions and recommendations and described actions underway to address our recommendations as well as efforts being taken to reduce travel costs for the current fiscal year. While agreeing with our recommendations, DOI stated that it took exception to certain statements in our report. We address DOI's concerns by referring to the relevant points made in our report and reaffirming our position in the "Agency Comments and Our Evaluation" section.

## BACKGROUND

The National Park System of the United States comprises 385 areas covering around 84 million acres in 49 states, the District of Columbia, American Samoa, Guam, Puerto Rico, Saipan, and the Virgin Islands. Besides running the National Park System, the Park Service fills many other roles to augment the conservation and the preservation of natural resources.

In its mission, the Park Service recognizes its responsibility for managing a great variety of national and international programs designed to help extend the benefits of natural and cultural resources conservation and outdoor recreation throughout the nation and the world. Implementation of its domestic and global missions and leadership roles presents opportunities for recurrent travel.

OIA provides the overall framework for the Park Service's international programs and coordinates its participation in international activities in fulfillment of global obligations and domestic legislative requirements. OIA also has responsibility to ensure that Park Service employees comply with the *Federal Travel Regulation* and DOI foreign travel regulations as well as Park Service regulations when traveling outside the United States on official government business. AOC, the Park Service's consolidated administrative accounting and payment office, produces the Park Service's travel policies based on the *Federal Travel Regulation* and DOI travel regulations. DOI has adopted the *Federal Travel Regulation* and its supplements and amendments

---

*Financial Management Systems Requirements* that describe the requirements of the Federal Financial Management Improvement Act of 1996. See Joint Financial Management Improvement Program, *Travel System Requirements*, JFMIP-SR-99-9 (Washington, D.C.: July 1999).

as its basic travel and transportation policy for all its bureaus and offices, including the Park Service.

## OBJECTIVES, SCOPE, AND METHODOLOGY

We were asked to determine (1) whether the Park Service could provide its travel cost by type (such as foreign or domestic) and purpose (such as conference attendance or training) for fiscal years 1999, 2000, 2001, and 2002, and if not, what factors contribute to the Park Service's inability to provide the information, (2) the annual total travel costs for those years, and (3) how many foreign trips were authorized for those 4 fiscal years and at what estimated cost. We were also asked to describe the authorization procedures required for foreign travel.

In order to fulfill the first objective, we asked the Park Service to provide travel cost data from its travel accounting system for fiscal years 1999 through 2002. We requested the data for each of the Park Service's established regions. We identified the requirements for tracking and recording detailed travel data by reviewing the *Federal Travel Regulation*; JFMIP's *Travel System Requirements*; and DOI's and the Park Service's travel regulations, policies, and procedures. We identified the causes leading to the Park Service's inability to provide reliable detailed travel information that is consistent with the *Federal Travel Regulation* by interviewing Park Service officials and staff members, as well as certain DOI staff members. We visited the Park Service AOC and observed as travel vouchers were processed through the travel accounting system to gain an understanding of how travel cost data are processed and to ascertain the capabilities of the system. In addition, we interviewed an official at GSA responsible for gathering detailed travel information from certain agencies biennially and reviewed the travel information for fiscal year 2000 submitted to GSA by the Park Service to confirm the assertions that the Park Service used estimated, not actual, data in fulfilling the reporting requirement to GSA.

For objective two, we used the data given to us by the Park Service and adjusted for inflation. We reviewed the Park Service's financial statement audit for fiscal years 2000 and 2001 to determine if any identified material internal control weaknesses or reportable conditions could affect the reliability of the Park Service's travel data. We compared the total reported travel costs with the Park Service's reported outlays in each of the fiscal years and interviewed Park Service officials about the accuracy of the data. We compiled subtotals for the regional offices, as well as for the service centers and the Job Corps Program combined, and reconciled those subtotals with travel cost totals by fiscal year. We adjusted all dollar values for general inflation, using the Gross Domestic Product price index for all items with fiscal year 2001 as the base year.

Because the Park Service could not provide the actual cost of foreign travel, in order to fulfill the third objective, we asked the Park Service's OIA to provide the number of authorized foreign trips, and the cost estimates for related travel, which were both based on preauthorized amounts submitted to OIA on Foreign Travel Certification Forms (DI-1175). With certain limitations as discussed in the report, these data would be the best available to provide some indication of the level of foreign travel. We adjusted all dollar values for general inflation, using the Gross Domestic Product price index for all items with fiscal year 2001 as the base year.

To describe the Park Service's foreign travel authorization process, we obtained and reviewed applicable policy and procedures and other guidance on the foreign travel authorization process. This included the *Federal Travel Regulation*, the *Park Service International Travel Policies and Procedures*, and the *Park Service Temporary Duty Travel Policies*. Further, we discussed the applicable policies, procedures, and practices with appropriate Park Service officials, including headquarters officials in the Park Service OIA, AOC, and the offices of Parks Facility Management and Cultural Resource Stewardship and Partnerships.

# THE PARK SERVICE CANNOT DETERMINE ITS FOREIGN TRAVEL COSTS OR ITS TRAVEL COSTS FOR ATTENDING CONFERENCES

The Park Service does not know its actual costs for foreign travel or the travel costs related to attending conferences. This is because its systems and processes do not consistently or routinely record this information, although they are required to do so.

The *Federal Travel Regulation* requires that agencies capture certain data elements for processing federal travel expenditures. These data elements include type of travel, such as foreign or domestic, and travel purpose,[5] such as site visit, training attendance, or conference attendance. DOI and Park

---

[5] The travel purpose identifiers described in Appendix C of Chapter 301 of the *Federal Travel Regulation* are site visit, information meeting, training attendance, speech or presentation, conference attendance, relocation, and entitlement travel.

Service travel regulations similarly require tracking travel type and purpose. In addition, the Park Service's foreign travel policies and procedures specify that foreign travel be kept to the absolute minimum necessary for achieving its mission and objectives.

The Park Service's current system of processing travel vouchers and recording travel expenditures includes a combination of both centralized and decentralized functions. Airfare and other transportation costs, such as rental cars, are centrally billed to the Park Service AOC, and recorded in the aggregate as domestic travel, even though some of the transportation charges on a given invoice may be for foreign travel. A travel voucher claiming reimbursement for costs for transportation, lodging, meals, and other incidentals can be processed at the traveler's local park office and paid with a third-party draft,[6] or the voucher can be sent to AOC, where it is forwarded electronically to Treasury for reimbursement to the employee.[7]

Park Service officials told us that its current travel accounting system is limited in the amount of travel-related information it can preserve when processing certain valid payment methods, including third-party drafts. While travel type and purpose information may or may not be captured and retained at all park offices, AOC officials told us that they do not receive this travel information from the local offices or regions in enough detail to satisfy the *Federal Travel Regulation* requirement. For those travel vouchers processed at AOC, we noted that the current system has the capacity to record the travel type and purpose, but those data fields were not consistently being completed in processing individual vouchers.

Although the Park Service's foreign travel policies and procedures require that all foreign travel vouchers be sent to AOC for payment, AOC officials told us that some Park Service field offices may be paying foreign travel vouchers locally rather than submitting them to AOC. There is some risk of this occurring because we found no procedures in place to ensure that all foreign travel vouchers are sent to AOC for payment. Enforcement of this policy would not automatically yield summary information on foreign travel costs under the existing travel accounting system in view of the weaknesses discussed above; however, it could facilitate the enhancements necessary for tracking and monitoring Park Service foreign travel costs.

---

[6] A third-party draft payment system is an alternative payment system approved by the Department of the Treasury for imprest-fund-type transactions. A draft agent issues the draft after receiving the proper documentation and appropriate accounting information. The draft is drawn on a third-party draft contractor's account, and is issued to a vendor or employee for payment of goods and services, including travel-related costs.

[7] A third-party draft may only be used provided that the voucher is for $2,500 or less.

The Park Service is presently implementing a new end-to-end travel management system that its officials represented as fully compliant with the *Federal Travel Regulation*. When implemented, the new system will be able to provide travel information such as the number of foreign trips and conference attendance. However, this system is not expected to be operational throughout the Park Service until approximately September 2003.

The Federal Financial Management Improvement Act of 1996 requires, among other things, that agencies implement and maintain financial management systems that substantially comply with federal financial management systems requirements. These apply to existing systems in operation and new systems planned or under development. These system requirements are detailed in the *Financial Management Systems Requirements* series issued by JFMIP and in Office of Management and Budget Circular A-127, *Financial Management Systems*. JFMIP requirement documents identify (1) a framework for financial management systems, (2) core financial management systems requirements, and (3) 16 other financial and mixed systems supporting agency operations, of which the travel system is one. In 1999, JFMIP issued its *Travel System Requirements*, which defines mandatory and value-added functional requirements for system administration and major elements of the travel process. Mandatory requirements describe what the system must do and outline the minimum acceptable functionality necessary to establish a system. The capability to capture required standard data elements contained in the *Federal Travel Regulation* is considered a mandatory requirement.

In the absence of reliable detailed travel expense information such as travel type and purpose, the Park Service and the Congress have limited information available to determine whether funds appropriated for travel are being used effectively. In addition, GSA is limited in its efforts to collect information on the use of federal travel dollars for the purpose of developing cost-effective management practices governmentwide. For example, as required by 5 U.S.C. 5707(c), GSA directs each federal agency with more than $5 million in travel costs in a fiscal year to submit a biennial report detailing such information as total travel costs, costs of foreign and domestic travel, and costs of travel by varying purpose. While the Park Service has submitted this type of information to GSA in the past, many of the responses were based on estimates because the Park Service system does not capture all the required data elements. Therefore, the accuracy and reliability of the data it submits to GSA are questionable.

## TOTAL REPORTED TRAVEL COSTS
## HAVE INCREASED ANNUALLY

After adjusting for inflation, total reported travel costs at the Park Service in the past 3 years have increased by almost 29 percent, from approximately $39 million in fiscal year 1999 to approximately $50 million in fiscal year 2002. Total reported travel costs for fiscal years 2000 and 2001 were $45 million and $47 million, respectively. Figure 1 further illustrates the increased travel costs reported by the Park Service, which rose by 12 percent from fiscal year 1999 to fiscal year 2000, 4 percent from fiscal year 2000 to fiscal year 2001, and 7 percent from fiscal year 2001 to fiscal year 2002, or an average of 9 percent annually over the 3-year interval.

Table 1 depicts the total reported travel costs for fiscal years 1999 through 2002, for the Park Service's seven geographical regions, the Washington, D.C., office, and three remaining reporting units. As indicated in the table, travel costs for the Washington, D.C., office have increased by approximately 60 percent, increasing from $5.6 million in fiscal year 1999 to over $9 million in fiscal year 2002. Reported travel costs for the seven regional offices combined increased by approximately 26 percent, from almost $31 million in fiscal year 1999 to almost $39 million in fiscal year 2002. The three remaining units, which include the service centers and the Job Corps Program, showed a slight decrease in reported travel costs, going from almost $2.5 million in fiscal year 1999 to almost $2.4 million in fiscal year 2002.

In commenting on a draft of this report, DOI stated that the sharp increase in travel costs for the Washington, D.C., office from fiscal years 2001 to 2002 is primarily attributable to enhanced security measures in the wake of the events of September 11, 2001. During the course of our review or in its comments on our report, DOI did not provide any further information supporting its position. Without systems and processes in place that can track and record all pertinent travel related data, it is difficult for the agency to readily justify and document unusual variances and trends in Park Service employee official travel.

**Figure 1:** Park Service Reported Total Travel Costs, Fiscal Years 1999-2002, Actual and Adjusted for Inflation to 2001 Dollars

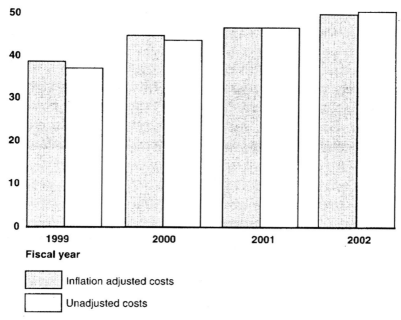

Note: This figure represents GAO's analysis of data provided by the Park Service.

## ALTERNATIVE DATA INDICATE THAT FOREIGN TRAVEL HAS INCREASED ANNUALLY

Given the Park Service's failure to record and thus inability to confidently report actual foreign trips and the related costs, the Park Service's OIA provided us estimated trip and cost data, based on authorization documents supplemented by a database it uses to track the whereabouts, health, and safety of Park Service employees traveling outside of the continental United States. OIA receives travel authorization documents, including estimated costs for foreign travel, approximately 6 weeks prior to a Park Service employee initiating such travel.

**Table 1:** Total Travel Costs by Region, Fiscal Years 1999-2002

Amounts in 2001 dollars

| Region | Total travel costs reported by the Park Service | | | |
|---|---|---|---|---|
| | 1999 | 2000 | 2001 | 2002 |
| Alaska Region | $2,596,218 | $3,410,092 | $3,349,905 | $3,270,865 |
| Intermountain | 7,564,609 | 9,025,026 | 9,291,335 | 9,354,515 |
| Mid-Atlantic Region | 4,394,316 | 5,007,060 | 5,525,627 | 5,896,676 |
| Mid-West Region | 3,650,768 | 3,997,144 | 4,260,674 | 4,270,640 |
| National Capital Region | 1,440,532 | 1,539,385 | 1,488,933 | 1,562,141 |
| Pacific West Region | 6,620,250 | 7,844,150 | 8,001,775 | 8,793,542 |
| South East Region | 4,379,039 | 5,399,325 | 5,559,439 | 5,399,628 |
| **Subtotal** | **$30,645,732** | **$36,222,182** | **$37,477,688** | **$38,548,007** |
| Washington, D.C. | $5,585,035 | $5,970,306 | $6,733,938 | $9,030,333 |
| Denver Service Center | $1,824,702 | $1,968,331 | $1,781,823 | $1,593,143 |
| Harpers Ferry Center | 646,873 | 717,459 | 651,599 | 635,483 |
| Job Corps Program | 21,331 | 9,582 | 91,097 | 136,076 |
| **Subtotal** | **$2,492,906** | **$2,695,372** | **$2,524,519** | **$2,364,702** |
| **Total** | **$38,723,673** | **$44,887,860** | **$46,736,145** | **$49,943,042** |

Source: GAO.
Note: Dollars are adjusted to 2001 dollars. This figure represents GAO's analysis of data provided by the Park Service.

The OIA information indicates that the number of trips authorized for foreign travel increased by approximately 32 percent, rising steadily from 355 trips in fiscal year 1999 to 470 trips in fiscal year 2002. Total pretravel estimated costs for these trips increased from $488,830 in fiscal year 1999 to $652,236 in fiscal year 2002 (adjusted for inflation), indicating that foreign travel costs may have increased by about a third during this 3-year interval. There were 379 authorized trips for fiscal year 2000 at an estimated cost of $639,345, and 442 authorized trips in fiscal year 2001, at an estimated cost of $641,395. OIA does not verify that the authorized travel actually took place, track actual costs in the event of a trip being extended or shortened since approval, or determine whether reimbursements were received where costs are shared by a host country or organization. Appendix I provides further details on the estimated foreign travel information compiled by OIA and the information is arranged by regional office, with one total for all remaining park offices.

## FOREIGN TRAVEL AUTHORIZATION PROCEDURES INCLUDE MULTIPLE LEVELS OF APPROVAL

OIA evaluates opportunities and coordinates responses involving the Park Service in international programs, projects, and activities. In addition, OIA is designated to ensure implementation of federal, DOI, and Park Service foreign travel procedures and regulations. Consistent with DOI policy, OIA policy states that the number of travelers and the number and length of trips to foreign countries are to be held to the absolute minimum necessary for conducting essential business and accomplishing established Park Service objectives.

When a need to travel internationally is identified, either to attend a conference or meeting or to provide technical assistance, the employee must first obtain approval from his or her immediate supervisor by submitting a foreign travel certification form[8] and a justification memorandum. The supervisor is to review the documentation for consistency with Park Service program priorities and strategic planning goals, cost-effective accomplishment of Park Service mission, and fiscally responsible scheduling of the travel. The supervisor is to then determine if the costs can be met, and consider the impact of the employee's time away from work.

Upon supervisor approval, the required authorization forms are submitted to the employee's regional director[9] for approval, and then to OIA about 6 weeks prior to the proposed travel. OIA forwards the documents to the Park Service's Deputy Director, DOI's Assistant Director for Fish and Wildlife and Parks, and DOI's Office of International Affairs. Once all the agency approvals are received, OIA requests approval from the Department of State and the appropriate U.S. embassy. Travel may begin after all approvals are received.

## CONCLUSIONS

The Park Service lacks systems and procedures needed to capture and report travel cost in accordance with the *Federal Travel Regulation*. Specifically, it does not identify travel type, which would indicate travel to foreign countries versus domestic travel, nor does it identify travel purpose, which would indicate travel related to site visit, or conference attendance, for

---

[8] Form DI-1175, a DOI document.
[9] Approval by an associate director is required for Washington, D.C., office employees.

example. System inadequacies and a lack of adherence to policies and procedures contributed to the unavailability of reliable, detailed travel data consistent with *Federal Travel Regulation* requirements. The Park Service is in the process of implementing a new travel accounting system that is designed to track all required data elements under the *Federal Travel Regulation*. However, this system is not expected to be fully operational until approximately September 2003.

The Park Service's reported total travel costs have increased over the past 3 fiscal years. In addition, alternative data on foreign travel indicate that the number of authorized trips and the related costs for the same period have risen. Without reliable detailed historical travel information, such as foreign versus domestic travel cost, or travel costs by various purposes, the Park Service is limited in its ability to manage travel and transportation costs and the Congress has limited information available to determine whether funds appropriated for official travel are being used effectively.

## RECOMMENDATIONS FOR EXECUTIVE ACTION

We recommend that the Secretary of the Interior require the Director of the National Park Service to take the following actions:

- Establish procedures for capturing travel data, including travel type and purpose, as required by the *Federal Travel Regulation*.
- Enforce existing Park Service foreign travel policy requiring all foreign travel vouchers to be processed electronically by AOC to enable a complete and proper recording of foreign travel costs.
- Address JFMIP *Travel System Requirements* when designing and implementing the travel system scheduled for completion later this year as well as any future travel systems.

## AGENCY COMMENTS AND OUR EVALUATION

In its written comments, DOI concurred with our recommendations and described actions underway to address our recommendations. DOI also described efforts being taken to reduce travel costs for the current fiscal year. While agreeing with our recommendations, DOI stated that it took exception to certain statements in this report. First, DOI stated that our report implies foreign travel costs are partly to blame for the high travel costs reported, when in fact foreign travel comprises a small part of the Park Service's total travel costs. Our report does not make any observations on the significance of foreign travel costs in relation to total travel costs. Further, the report states that the Park Service does not know its actual foreign travel costs for the periods we reviewed and therefore, it would not have been possible for us to make any such observations.

Second, DOI stated that the number of estimated foreign trips in our report was misleading. It stated that approximately 50 percent of the total number of foreign trips shown in our report was actually across-the-border travel to either Mexico or Canada, and thereby exempt from the required Foreign Travel Certification Form (DI-1175). Our report provides the total number of estimated foreign trips during the period under review based on the Park Service's reported information. In addition, DOI's comment regarding exemption from filing form DI-1175 for across-the-border travel is not accurate. The Park Service's International Travel Policies and Procedures explicitly require that a DI-1175 be filed for travel to both Mexico and Canada. For these reasons, our report does not differentiate between trips to our bordering countries from trips to any others. Further, the estimated numbers of foreign trips in our report were obtained by reviewing approved forms DI-1175.

DOI commented that the Park Service was able to provide supporting documentation related to foreign travel. However, as discussed in the report, the Park Service could not provide its actual foreign travel costs for the periods under review. The estimated trip and cost data provided by OIA from the forms DI-1175 cannot be referred to as supporting documentation for actual foreign travel costs incurred because of the caveats identified in this report.

Finally, regarding travel purpose, such as training or conference attendance, DOI noted that the report did not state that the Park Service already captures the purpose for foreign travel. Our report points out that the travel accounting system has the capacity to record travel type and purpose, but notes that those data fields were not consistently being completed in processing individual vouchers, which resulted in the Park Service being unable to provide us with the requested data. Thus, this data is captured for some travel, but it is not consistently recorded in the Park Service's travel accounting system in a manner that would facilitate routine and comprehensive reporting of such data.

# APPENDIX I. APPENDIXES NATIONAL PARK SERVICE'S AUTHORIZED FOREIGN TRIPS AND ESTIMATED TRAVEL COSTS APPENDIX I

The following are estimated foreign travel costs, adjusted for inflation, by fiscal year for the seven National Park Service (Park Service) regions, the Washington, D.C., office, and all parks in total.

**Table 2:** Estimated Foreign Travel Costs, for Each Region, the Washington, D.C., Office, and Parks Aggregated, Fiscal Years 1999-2002

| Amount in 2001 dollars | | | | |
|---|---|---|---|---|
| | Park Service estimates of foreign travel costs | | | |
| Region | 1999 | 2000 | 2001 | 2002 |
| Alaska Region | $46,393 | 0 | $18,210 | $17,635 |
| Intermountain Region | 29,486 | 39,821 | 13,334 | 5,833 |
| Mid-Atlantic Region | 4,508 | 15,479 | 30,129 | 23,495 |
| Mid-West Region | 5,405 | 23,830 | 24,066 | 14,305 |
| National Capital Region | 0 | 3,289 | 2,430 | 5,577 |
| Pacific West Region | 27,485 | 20,951 | 34,594 | 27,760 |
| South East Region | 5,733 | 23,085 | 7,470 | 4,053 |
| **Subtotal regional offices** | **$119,010** | **$126,455** | **$130,233** | **$98,658** |
| Washington, D.C. | $139,135 | $161,297 | $131,107 | $110,910 |
| All parks | $230,685 | $351,595 | $380,054 | $442,668 |
| **Total** | **$488,830** | **$639,347** | **$641,394** | **$652,236** |
| Number of trips | 355 | 379 | 442 | 470 |

Source: GAO.

Note: This table represents GAO's analysis of data provided by the Park Service's Office of International Affairs.

As of September 30, 2002, there were about 27 foreign trips already authorized for fiscal year 2003, at an estimated cost of $43,334, adjusted to reflect 2001 dollars.

*Chapter 10*

# NATIONAL PARK SERVICE: EFFORTS UNDERWAY TO ADDRESS ITS MAINTENANCE BACKLOG[*]

## *Barry T. Hill*

### INTRODUCTION

In 2002, GAO reported that the design of the National Park Service's new asset management process was complete but implementation was just beginning. The new process will address deferred maintenance, commonly referred to as the maintenance backlog, as part of a much broader approach to its asset management. When fully developed and implemented, the new process will, for the first time, enable the agency to have a (1) reliable inventory of its assets; (2) process for reporting on the condition of the assets in its inventory; and (3) consistent, systemwide methodology for estimating the deferred maintenance costs for its assets. As a result, agency managers and the Congress should receive much more accurate and reliable information on the amount of deferred maintenance needs throughout the national park system. Nonetheless, while the Park Service's current efforts are promising, GAO reported on a few areas that the agency needed to address to improve the performance of the process. These included the need

[*] Excerpted from CRS Report GAO-03-1177T. September 27, 2003.

to (1) develop costs and schedules for completing the implementation of the process, (2) better coordinate the tracking of the process among Park Service headquarters units to avoid duplication of effort within the agency; and, (3) better define its approach to determine the condition of its assets, and how much the assessments will cost.

Since that report, the agency appears to have made progress. While the complete implementation of the process will not occur until fiscal year 2006, the agency has completed, or is nearing completion of, a number of substantial and important steps. According to the Park Service, the agency has completed its asset inventory and trained staff on the use of the required computer software. In addition, the Park Service provided information indicating that it was addressing each of the concerns identified in GAO's 2002 report. Specifically, the Park Service (1) developed cost and schedule estimates for the complete implementation of the process, (2) developed a plan with an implementation schedule to eliminate any duplication or inconsistencies between organizational components, and (3) completed annual condition assessments—visual inspections—on all but nine of the larger parks in the system for which it only plans to perform a more comprehensive condition assessment. According to the Park Service, the work done so far are necessary steps and reflect some of the best practices of the private sector in developing and implementing an effective facility management process.

GAO, the Department of the Interior, and others have reported on the National Park Service's efforts to develop an effective maintenance management process that would, among other things, enable the agency to accurately and reliably estimate the amount of deferred maintenance on its assets. Over the years, the agency's estimates of the cost of its deferred maintenance have varied widely— sometimes by billions of dollars. Currently, the agency estimates that its deferred maintenance backlog will cost over $5 billion. In April 2002, GAO reported on the status of efforts to develop better deferred maintenance data.

# RESULTS IN BRIEF

The Park Service's new asset management process is designed to address deferred maintenance, commonly referred to as the maintenance backlog, as part of a much broader approach to asset management. When fully and properly implemented, the new process is expected, for the first time, to enable the agency to have a (1) reliable inventory of its assets; (2)

process for reporting on the condition of each asset in its inventory; and (3) consistent, systemwide methodology for estimating the deferred maintenance costs for each asset. As a result, agency managers and the Congress should receive much more accurate and reliable information on the extent of deferred maintenance needs throughout the national park system. Nonetheless, while the Park Service's current efforts are promising, we reported on a few areas that the agency needed to address to improve the performance of the process. These included the need to (1) develop costs and schedules for completing the implementation of the process so that the agency's performance could be monitored and assessed, (2) better coordinate the tracking of the process among Park Service headquarters units to avoid duplication of effort within the agency, and (3) better define its approach to assessing the condition of its assets, and determining how much the assessments will cost.

Since our report last year, I am pleased to say that the agency appears to have made progress. While complete implementation of the process will not occur until fiscal year 2006, the agency has completed, or nearly completed, several substantial and important steps. According to the Park Service, it has completed its asset inventory, trained staff on the use of the required computer software, and completed most of the on-site inspections necessary to determine the condition and maintenance needs of inventoried assets. In addition, the Park Service provided information indicating that it was addressing each of the concerns identified in our prior report.

## BACKGROUND

The national park system contains 388 park units. These park units have a diverse inventory of facilities and other assets, including over 18,000 permanent structures, 8,000 miles of roads, 1,800 bridges and tunnels, 4,400 housing units, about 700 water and wastewater systems, over 400 dams, and 200 solid waste operations. The Park Service values these assets at over $35 billion. Needless to say, the proper care and maintenance of the national parks and their supporting infrastructure is essential to the continued use and enjoyment of our national treasures by this and future generations. However, for years Park Service officials have highlighted the agency's inability to keep up with its maintenance needs. In this connection, Park Service officials and others have often cited a continuing buildup of unmet maintenance needs as evidence of deteriorating conditions throughout the national park system. The accumulation of these unmet needs is commonly

referred to as its "maintenance backlog." Although the Park Service has
spent almost two decades and about $11 million addressing this problem, it
still does not have a reliable estimate of deferred maintenance needs for its
facilities and other assets.

In the past several years, concerns about the cost of operating and
maintaining federal recreation sites within the National Park Service, as well
as other federal land management agencies, led the Congress to provide a
significant new source of funds. This additional source of funding—the
Recreational Fee Demonstration Program[1]—was, in part, aimed at helping
the agencies address their backlogged repair and maintenance problems. This
new funding source is in addition to annual appropriations the Park Service
receives each year for maintenance activities.[2]

Despite the years of attention and funding and the well-intended efforts
of the agency and the Congress to resolve the maintenance backlog dilemma,
it has not gone away. While Congress continues to provide hundreds of
millions of dollars annually to deal with the maintenance backlog at the
national parks, the Park Service still has no reliable data on the size of the
problem, raising questions about what has been accomplished with the
provided funds.

## WHEN FULLY AND PROPERLY IMPLEMENTED, THE PARK SERVICE'S NEW ASSET MANAGEMENT PROCESS SHOULD PROVIDE ACCURATE AND RELIABLE DEFERRED MAINTENANCE DATA

As we reported in April 2002, the Park Service has made progress in
developing a new asset management process that, when fully and properly
implemented, should provide the agency with more accurate and reliable
estimates of the amount of deferred maintenance of its assets. As currently
planned, the new process will, for the first time, enable the agency to have a
(1) reliable inventory of its assets; (2) process for reporting on the condition

[1] Since fiscal year 1996, the Park Service, as well as three other federal land management
agencies, have been authorized to have a fee demonstration program. Under this temporary
program, the agencies are permitted to experiment with increased and/or new recreation fees.
The revenue generated from this program remains available for agency use to address a
variety of needs, including maintenance, without further appropriation.
[2] The House Committee on Appropriations has stressed that recreation fees should never be used
to replace appropriated funds; the fees should be used for direct improvements on site that
enhance the recreation experience. H.R. Rep. No. 106-646 (2000).

of assets in its inventory; and (3) systemwide methodology for estimating deferred maintenance costs for assets.

The new asset management process is composed of both systemwide, integrated software to track cost and maintenance data and regular condition assessments of Park Service assets. The cornerstone of the new asset management process is the Facility Management Software System. This cradle-to-grave asset and work management process will allow park, regional office, or Park Service headquarters managers to track when, what, and how much maintenance and related costs has been directed at each specific asset.

In addition to using the software system, the Park Service plans to assess the condition of its assets. These assessments will be inspections to document the condition of an asset as measured against applicable maintenance or condition standards. There are two types of condition assessments—annual and comprehensive. Annual assessments are essentially "eyeball inspections" of facilities to identify obvious and apparent deficiencies. Comprehensive assessments are more in-depth inspections to identify less obvious deficiencies, such as foundation or structural problems. While the eye-ball assessments are annual, the comprehensive assessments, which are much more expensive and timeconsuming, occur in 5-year cycles. The Park Service is to use the information obtained from these condition assessments to establish the overall condition of a facility or asset, including the resources needed to address its deferred maintenance needs and future facility needs. The cost of identified deferred maintenance needs will be estimated using another computer software system that will provide a uniform method for estimating repair and maintenance costs for each asset in the inventory. Agency managers will use the condition assessment information in combination with an asset priority ranking system to set priorities for deferred maintenance projects.

While the design of the new process is complete, we reported in April 2002 that the Park Service had just begun implementing it. For example, at that time, the agency was still inventorying its assets and training staff on how to use the new process at about a third of the park units in the national park system. We reported that because managers at each park will be required to implement this new process using a uniform systemwide methodology, the resulting deferred maintenance estimates should permit agency managers, as well as the Congress, to monitor progress in reducing deferred maintenance both at the individual park and systemwide levels. However, we noted that while the new process is promising, its success cannot be determined until staff in each of the park units are trained and the new asset management process is fully and properly implemented.

In our last report, we also raised three concerns about the Park Service's implementation of the new asset management process. While these matters were not significant enough to undermine the overall merit of the new process, we believed that addressing them would improve the effectiveness of the process. First, even though the Park Service had been developing its new process for more than 3 years, it had not yet estimated its total implementation costs or developed a schedule for completing implementation. While the agency had made progress in developing schedules and costs for some components of the process, it had not yet estimated when it will complete all the required condition assessments or what they will cost. We noted that monitoring and assessing performance against budgets and time frames would be difficult without complete estimates and schedules that include all components of the process, including the completion of condition assessments.

Second, two different operating divisions within the Park Service—Concessions Management and Facilities Management—were developing separate processes for tracking and reporting deferred maintenance, even though both units are responsible for managing the condition of government-owned facilities. Because both of these units have similar responsibilities, it seemed reasonable that they would work together in a coordinated way to ensure that their efforts are not duplicative.

Finally, the Park Service reported that about one-third of the park units were to complete annual condition assessments by the end of fiscal year 2002. We noted that this approach may be appropriate for meeting programmatic and financial reporting needs in the short term; however, without comprehensive assessments, this approach might result in overlooking more complex and costly problems in the long term. As a result, this approach could understate the extent of the deferred maintenance problem. Park Service officials told us that the agency eventually planned to conduct comprehensive assessments for all assets. However, at the time they had not developed a plan detailing where, when, and how the assessments will be done or what they will cost.

# The Park Service Has Made Progress Implementing its Asset Management Process Since Our Last Report

Although full implementation of the new asset management process is still years from completion, the Park Service appears to have made progress since our last report. Also, importantly, Park Service management has demonstrated its commitment to implementing this process by withholding some fiscal year 2003 funding from parks that are not complying with the agency's implementation goals.

The agency now reports that it has completed its inventory of assets for all park units as well as the first round of staff training on the use of the facilities management software. The agency also contracted with a consulting firm to evaluate its training and implementation efforts to help ensure that the training is effective and that the software system is being consistently applied throughout the park system. The Park Service has analyzed the firm's results and is now developing a training curriculum to address the firm's recommendations. The Park Service expects to begin implementing the training in January or February 2004.

The agency is also addressing each of the issues raised in our last report. Specifically, the Park Service has now developed cost and schedule estimates for the complete implementation of the process. According to the schedule, the process is to be fully implemented by the end of fiscal year 2006, when all the comprehensive condition assessments are complete for all park units and deferred maintenance and other needs can be estimated on a reliable and consistent basis for assets throughout the national park system. The Park Service estimates now that the cost of the complete rollout and implementation, including performing condition assessments, will be about $91 million from fiscal years 1999 through 2006. Thereafter, it estimates that the annual costs of sustaining the process once it is fully operational will be about $20 million.

In response to our concern that two different operating divisions within the agency—Concessions Management and Facilities Management—were developing separate processes for maintaining government-owned facilities, the Park Service told us that they agreed and are committed to implementing a single facilities management process. According to the agency, it has developed a plan with an implementation schedule to eliminate any duplication or inconsistencies between these two components of the organization.

The Park Service has also made progress in performing its servicewide facility condition assessments. According to the Park Service, it has completed annual condition assessments—visual inspections—on all but nine of the larger parks in the system.[3] In addition, the Park Service is concurrently performing the more detailed, comprehensive condition assessments on other park units. According to the Park Service, the work done so far are necessary steps and reflect some of the best practices of the private sector in developing and implementing an effective facility management process.

## CONCLUSION

The Park Service has a solemn responsibility to take care of the nation's natural, cultural and historic treasures. While it has unfortunately taken decades to achieve the current level of focus on maintaining these treasures, the Park Service apparently now has made substantive progress in developing and implementing a system it can use to determine the conditions of the assets in its portfolio and develop accurate and reliable estimates of its deferred maintenance needs. However, the agency has not yet completed the task. Determining the assets' conditions and their maintenance costs will require years of sustained commitment by the agency and by the Congress to ensure that the full benefits of the agency's new facility management process are realized.

---

[3] In order to expedite the condition assessments, the Park Service decided to only complete the more comprehensive condition assessments on the nine larger parks. These parks include Appalachian Trail, Delaware Water Gap, Gateway, Golden Gate, Grand Canyon, Great Smoky Mountains, Rocky Mountain, Yellowstone, and Yosemite. By the end of fiscal year 2003, the Park Service will have completed these assessments for five of the nine parks with the remaining four to be completed by the end of fiscal year 2004.

# Chapter 11

# SOUTH FLORIDA ECOSYSTEM RESTORATION AND THE COMPREHENSIVE EVERGLADES RESTORATION PLAN[*]

## *Nicole T. Carter*

## INTRODUCTION

The Everglades, a unique network of subtropical wetlands, is now half its original size. Many factors have contributed to its decline, including flood control projects and agricultural and urban development. As part of a larger restoration program for South Florida, the U.S. Army Corps of Engineers (Corps) and other federal, state, tribal, and local agencies collaborated to develop a Comprehensive Everglades Restoration Plan (CERP or the plan). CERP focuses on increasing storage of wet season waters to provide more water during the dry season for the natural system and urban and agricultural users. The plan consists of 68 projects estimated to take 36 years and $7.8 billion to complete. The Water Resources Development Act of 2000 (P.L.106-541) authorizes appropriations for initial construction projects and their operation and maintenance. The federal government will pay half the

---

[*] Excerpted from CRS Report RS20702. Updated January 27, 2003.

plan's costs and an array of state, tribal, and local agencies the other half. Major issues associated with the plan include: development of programmatic regulations, timely completion, coordination of restoration efforts, effectiveness of restoration efforts, uncertainties in technologies and costs, specifics of water allocation, and effect on the Corps budget. Final programmatic regulations are expected early in 2003. This report outlines the history and current conditions of the Everglades, CERP legislation and funding, and associated issues.

## INTRODUCTION

The Water Resources Development Act of 2000 (Title VI, P.L. 106-541) authorized involvement of the U.S. Army Corps of Engineers (Corps) in a plan to restore the Everglades. Programmatic regulations are being developed to define the processes and procedures that will guide the 35-year implementation of the Comprehensive Everglades Restoration Plan (CERP or the plan). The Everglades is the defining component of the South Florida ecosystem (see Figure 1), which incorporates 16 national wildlife refuges and four national park units. South Florida is also home to more than six million people and a large agricultural economy. There is wide agreement that major changes in water quantity, quality, timing, and distribution since the 1950s have significantly degraded the region's ecological health. During the dry season, the current water regime in South Florida is unable to provide sufficient freshwater supplies to meet the needs of the natural system and urban and agricultural consumers. Water shortages are expected to become more frequent as demand by urban and agricultural consumers increases.

## EVERGLADES HISTORY

The Everglades is a network of subtropical wetland landscapes that once stretched 220 miles from Orlando to Florida Bay. Several hundred lakes fed slow-moving creeks, called sloughs, that joined the Kissimmee River. Depending on rainfall, water flowed south down the river or topped the river's banks and flowed through 40,000 acres of marsh to Lake Okeechobee. During the summer rainy season, the lake would overflow its southern shore, spilling water into the Everglades. Due to flat topography, this water moved slowly south to Florida Bay through a shallow 40-mile wide, 100-mile long sawgrass marsh. These wetlands acted as natural filters and retention areas that recharged underlying aquifers. The unique habitat resulting from the Everglades' combination of abundant moisture, rich soils, and subtropical temperatures supported a vast array of species. However, by the mid-1800s, many in South Florida viewed the Everglades as an unproductive swamp. Flood control and reclamation efforts that manipulated the Everglades hydrology promoted development of the East Coast of Florida and permitted agriculture on reclaimed marshland. Principal among the human interventions affecting the Everglades is the Corps' Central and Southern Florida (C&SF) project, which was first authorized by Congress in 1948 to control floods and to satisfy other water management needs of South Florida. Water flows in South Florida are now directed by 1,000 miles of canals, 720 miles of levees, and almost 200 water control structures.

**Figure 1.** Principal Components of the South Florida Ecosystem

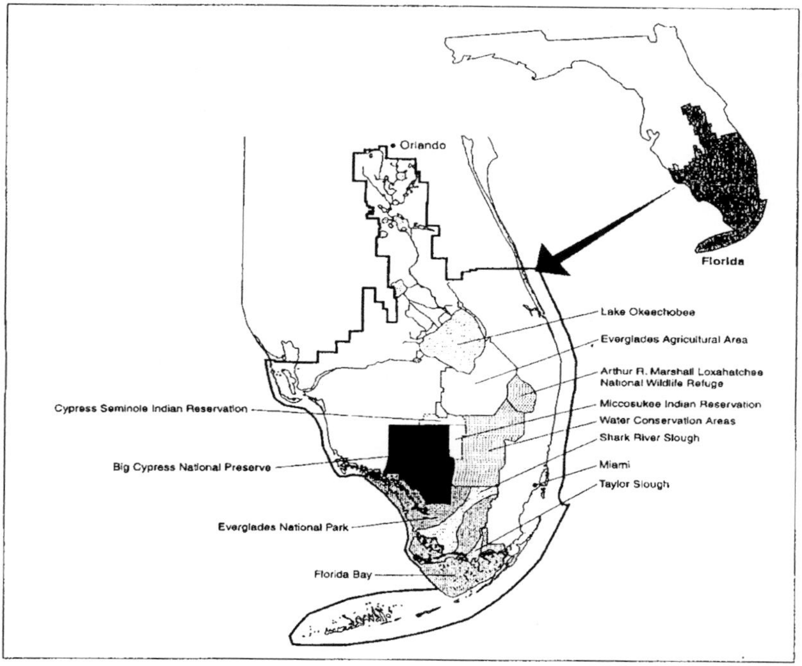

**Source:** Adapted from an illustration prepared by the South Florida Ecosystem Restoration Task Force.

# CURRENT CONDITIONS AND
# RECENT RESTORATION EFFORTS

Management and development activities have markedly changed the Everglades' water regime. The C&SF project redirects water that once flowed from Lake Okeechobee across the Everglades in a slow-moving sheet into canals and rivers discharging directly to the ocean. Experts now believe that the Everglades receives too little water during the dry season and too much during the rainy season. The altered water regime combined with urban and agricultural development have reduced the Everglades to half its original size. Habitat loss has threatened or endangered numerous plant and animal species.

The Everglades is also affected by degraded water quality. Pollutants from urban areas and agricultural runoff, including excess nutrients (such as phosphorous and nitrogen), metals, and pesticides, have harmed plant and animal populations. Nutrients entering the Everglades have caused a decline in native vegetation and an overabundance of invasive exotic species. Changes in the quantity, quality, and timing of freshwater flows have also disrupted the equilibrium of coastal estuaries and reef systems.

The federal government and the State of Florida have already undertaken many restoration activities, such as acquiring lands and preparing a multi-species recovery plan. Between FY1993 and FY2002, $1.7 billion in federal funds and $3.6 billion in state funds were appropriated for South Florida restoration. The South Florida Ecosystem Restoration Task Force, which was formalized by the Water Resources Development Act of 1996 (P.L. 104-303), coordinates the numerous restoration activities. The Task Force facilitates restoration using the following goals: (1) "get the water right," (2) restore, preserve, and protect natural habitats and species, and (3) foster compatibility of built and natural systems. It is estimated that achieving these goals for South Florida would cost $14.8 billion, of which $7.8 billion would be spent under CERP. This plan is the principal mechanism under the broader restoration program for "getting the water right," i.e., restoring natural hydrologic functions and water quality, and providing water supplies.

# COMPREHENSIVE EVERGLADES RESTORATION PLAN

CERP focuses on water quantity, quality, timing, and distribution. The overarching concept behind the plan is to capture and store freshwater currently discharged to the ocean to be used during the dry season; an estimated 80% of the captured water would be used for the natural system, and an estimated 20% for agricultural and urban uses. CERP calls for removing 240 miles of levees and canals, and building a network of reservoirs, underground storage wells, and pumping stations that would capture water and redistribute it to replicate natural flow.

## Legislation in the 106<sup>th</sup> Congress

Title VI of the Water Resources Development Act (WRDA) of 2000 approved CERP as contained in the "Final Integrated Feasibility Report and Programmatic Environmental Impact Statement" as modified by the Act. Passage followed years of delicate negotiations among federal agencies, the State of Florida, Congress, and disparate groups of stakeholders including local and national environmental organizations, sugar growers, utility companies, home builders, the Seminole Tribe of Florida, and the Miccosukee Tribe of Indians.

## Funding

Under Title VI, CERP construction as well as operation and maintenance costs are equally shared by Florida and the federal government.[1] Title VI authorizes four pilot projects at a total cost of $69 million ($34.5 million federal share), 10 construction projects and a monitoring program at a total cost of $1.1 billion ($550.5 million federal share), and modifications to the C&SF Project not to exceed $206 million ($103 million federal share). In total, the plan requires an estimated $7.8 billion—$5.5 billion for construction and $2.3 billion for necessary lands, easements, water rights, relocation expenses, and disposal areas. The Corps expects to request congressional authorization for additional projects every two years through 2014. In May 2000, Florida passed legislation approving CERP and committing $2 billion in state resources.

For CERP in FY2003, the Administration requested $37 million for

---

[1] Operation and maintenance costs are estimated at $172 million annually (1999 price levels) for the completed plan. Title VI departs from Section 528 of the Water Resources Development Act of 1996, which prohibits federal funding of operation and maintenance. Proponents of the exception argued that a federal project damaged the Everglades and much of the restoration will benefit federally-owned land.

Corps activities and $9 million for Department of Interior agencies.[2] The House and Senate versions of the Interior Appropriations bill provided the requested $9 million. The Corps' appropriations are included as part of the Central and Southern Florida line item in the Energy and Water Development Appropriations Act; that line item in the budget request totaled $108 million. The House and Senate Appropriations Committees (H.R. 5431, H.Rept. 107-681; S. 2784, S.Rept. 107-220) and the Stevens Amendment (in the nature of a substitute to the FY2003 Omnibus Appropriations Resolution H.J.Res. 2) recommended $96 million, $98 million, and $90 million, respectively. The Senate report and Stevens Amendment explained that the reduction resulted from questions raised about the implementation of the restoration project, specifically that it was too heavily weighted in favor of commercial development of water supplies rather than the restoration of the Everglades. Neither the Energy and Water Development Appropriations bill nor the Interior Appropriations bill for FY2003 has been enacted.

## CURRENT CERP ISSUES

While support for CERP has been rather broad, some reservations remain over the specifics of implementation. In particular, concerns have been raised regarding the allocation of water under the programmatic regulations that will guide CERP's implementation. Other issues include: coordination of activities; timely completion of CERP components; effectiveness of restoration efforts; uncertainties in technologies and their costs; and the Plan's effect on the Corps budget.

## PROGRAMMATIC REGULATIONS

The final programmatic regulations will define the processes and procedures that guide CERP implementation and operations. Section VI of WRDA 2000 required the promulgation of these regulations by December 2002. The Corps announced in December 2002 that it anticipates the final regulations in early 2003. The Corps presented draft versions in December

---

[2] More information on Corps funding is available in CRS Report RL31307, *Appropriations for FY2003: Energy and Water Development.* More information on Interior funding is available in CRS Report RL31306, *Appropriations for FY2003: Interior and Related Agencies.*

2001 and August 2002, which received comments from interested parties and the public. A few Members of the House and Senate submitted written comments on the 2002 draft.[3]

A major concern was the lack of a clearly stated proportion of the water generated by CERP that will benefit natural areas. Many want the often-discussed 80% allocation to restoration to be explicit in the programmatic regulations, while others feel that there are too many uncertainties to be that specific. Another issue was that some viewed the role of the Department of Interior as being unfairly relegated to one of consultation rather than concurring authority. Other expressed concerns were that interim goals should be adopted as part of the regulations when available and that the public outreach activities during implementation (particularly related to minorities) needed further development.

## Coordination

As evidenced by the concerns raised about the programmatic regulations regarding the status of the Department of the Interior, a significant challenge for CERP implementation will be coordination. The Corps leads CERP implementation with cooperation from local sponsors and several federal agencies: Department of the Interior (U.S. Fish and Wildlife Service, National Park Service, and U.S. Geological Survey), Department of Agriculture, and U.S. Environmental Protection Agency. Cooperating state entities are the South Florida Water Management District, the Florida Game and Fresh Water Fish Commission, and the Florida Department of Environmental Protection. The South Florida Ecosystem Restoration Task Force coordinates CERP's implementation with ongoing restoration efforts.[4] As CERP project details and operational policies (especially those related to the timing and delivery of water) are developed, support may shift and conflicts arise, testing the effectiveness of the coordination framework of CERP and the Task Force.

---

[3] For written comments by Members of Congress and other stakeholders [http://www. evergladesplan.org/pm/progr_regs_proposed_rule_comments.cfm].
[4] See U.S. General Accounting Office, *An Overall Strategic Plan and a Decision-Making Process Are Needed to Keep the Effort on Track,* RCED-99-121 (Washington, DC: April 1999).

## Timely Completion

There exists serious concern that delays or changes to related projects or CERP components may jeopardize the plan's feasibility. Current problems with acquiring land for the related Modified Water Deliveries Project is such an example. Without this land, the water flows needed to undertake CERP components on the eastern side of the Everglades National Park cannot be met. WRDA 2000 established that no funds for parts of CERP can be appropriated until the modified waters project is complete.

## Restoration Effectiveness

Some environmental groups question the extent to which CERP contributes to Everglades restoration and whether so complicated and costly a plan is necessary. There is also concern that the plan does not include enough measures to improve water quality in the Everglades. Some groups and federal agencies have expressed concern that CERP does not explicitly give natural systems precedence in water allocation, and that it is focused first on water supply rather than ecological restoration. To address this point, the Corps revised the project implementation sequencing to include restoration activities in earlier phases. These changes have not satisfied some groups and scientists who continue to oppose CERP. Some environmental groups, which support CERP and Florida's financial participation in the effort, have expressed concern about the source of Florida's contribution. They argue against using funds designated for the purchase of land needed for restoration to finance other types of CERP projects. These groups contend that land acquisition is essential for successful Everglades restoration.

## Technological and Cost Uncertainties

Because not all the scientific data and technologies to restore the South Florida ecosystem are available, CERP manages uncertainties using "adaptive assessment," which combines the implementation of initial project features with data collection for use in later project designs. The current state of knowledge and this adaptive assessment means that CERP is not as detailed as typical Corps feasibility proposals. Title VI authorizes funding of four pilot projects, including projects to test aquifer storage and recovery

(ASR), a technology that has never been used on such a large scale in these geologic conditions. ASR uses underground aquifers as reservoirs to store freshwater which will be withdrawn later during dry periods. A report by the National Research Council concluded that regional modeling efforts should precede implementation of ASR as proposed by CERP.[5] The report also noted the need to assess water quality standards of ASR water. A General Accounting Office (GAO) report identified uncertainties that could lead to changes in project designs and their costs.[6] These uncertainties included: (1) treatments required for water stored in aquifer storage and recovery wells, (2) adequacy of water quantity for Everglades National Park, and (3) phosphorous removal by storm water treatment areas.

## Corps Budget

The substantial commitment of federal funds to CERP might limit federal construction funds and the operation and maintenance funds available for other projects. The Corps' budget is of particular concern because of its backlog of construction projects and maintenance activities as well as its increased spending on security. Title VI requires that the annual federal budget include under the heading "Everglades Restoration" all proposed funding for the plan. Title VI also requires that the Corps budget show the total proposed funding for the plan and an assessment of the plan's impact on the budget year and long-term funding levels. Tracking these funds proves difficult because funding is included in both Interior and Energy and Water Appropriations bills.

---

[5] National Research Council, *Aquifer Storage and Recovery in the Comprehensive Everglades Restoration Plan*, (Washington, DC: February 2001).
[6] U.S. General Accounting Office. *Comprehensive Everglades Restoration Plan: Additional Water Quality Projects May Be Needed and Could Increase Costs*, RCED-00-235 (Washington, DC: September 2000).

# INDEX